EDUCATION IN A
DIVIDED WORLD

LONDON: GEOFFREY CUMBERLEGE

OXFORD UNIVERSITY PRESS

EDUCATION IN A DIVIDED WORLD

THE FUNCTION OF THE PUBLIC SCHOOLS
IN OUR UNIQUE SOCIETY

BY

James Bryant Conant

Harvard University Press

CAMBRIDGE, MASSACHUSETTS

1948

PRINTED AT THE HARVARD UNIVERSITY PRINTING OFFICE

CAMBRIDGE, MASSACHUSETTS, U.S.A.

To

GRACE RICHARDS CONANT

PREFACE

IN THE FALL of 1945 I had the privilege of giving three lectures at Teachers College, Columbia University, under the provisions of the Julius and Rosa Sachs Endowment Fund, to an audience composed of members of the faculty and the student body. The title of the series was "Public Education and the Structure of American Society," a subject on which I had planned someday to write a book. The authorities of Columbia kindly permitted me to reserve the right to expand my addresses at a later time and to publish them as I saw fit. The lectures were printed in the *Teachers College Record*. This fact enabled me to submit them to certain friends and acquaintances for frank criticism. The replies convinced me that something more drastic than revision and expansion was required. As a consequence the present volume, while based on the Sachs lectures of 1945, bears little resemblance to my discussion at Teachers College of high school and university problems.

The last three years have seen the publication of a number of noteworthy books on education. *Education for All American Youth* by the Educational Policies Commission, and *General Education in a Free Society* by a Harvard committee were available in 1945, and one of the Sachs lectures was devoted largely to showing that though differing in many respects the two volumes were in harmony in their basic recommendations. There soon followed several other books of importance, and the discussion of the problems of school and college in all these volumes as well as in professional journals made superfluous another treatment of the same subject addressed to educators. There did appear to be need, however, for a new appeal to the citizens of this country to interest themselves in the American system of public education. Many conversations over the years had convinced me of the existence of a widespread hostility to the public schools. This hostility was based on ignorance of the present practices in the schools and above all of the nature of the task they had been called upon to undertake. It was to be found as strongly among ardent supporters of the New Deal as among the most conservative opponents of the Roosevelt administration. The hostility was rarely to free tax-supported schools in theory, but rather to what was alleged to be the current situation; the comments were apt to be most vitriolic when professors of education and schools of education were blamed. With this attitude of many laymen in mind, I decided to alter the objective of my examination of public education and the structure of American society so as to make it the basis for a frank plea to the citizens of this republic to stop, look, and see their schools in operation, and consider the relation of the teachers' work to the future of this nation. Such is the purpose of this volume.

In the meantime, the international situation which to many appeared ambiguous in the fall of 1945 has become alarmingly clear and grim. The writings of various educators and the reports of educational committees, however, have not as yet reflected this clarification; rather they seem to have become less and less realistic as regards the foreign policy of the United States. Whatever may be one's political views, it seems hard to deny today that the relation of the United States to the struggle between the Soviet Union and the democracies has overriding significance for our national planning. The relevance of this struggle to our American system of free schools seems clear. Therefore, in various addresses in 1947 and early 1948 I have set forth the obvious interrelation between our American concept of democracy and the world-wide struggle. The substance of these addresses has been incorporated into the first two chapters of this book. Indeed, in the final construction of the volume I have used many portions of previous writings without shame. There is little to be found in the following pages which I have not said or written at some earlier time. On the other hand, no chapter is merely a reprint of an address or an article, for I have sought to make an integrated treatment of the various aspects of an educational and social philosophy which has been evolving some fifteen years.

I am indebted to so many people for assistance that it is impossible to name them. I owe a special debt of gratitude to the present Commissioner of Education of New York, Francis T. Spaulding, who as a member of the Harvard Faculty of Education first awakened my interest in the public schools. President Edmund E.

Day of Cornell and my other fellow-members of the Educational Policies Commission of the N.E.A. from 1940 to 1945 are responsible for my education in the problems of the tax-supported secondary schools. Of all those who criticized my Sachs lectures I should like to express my gratitude to those who took special pains and were unusually helpful: Professor H. A. Cowley of Stanford University, Professors Talcott Parsons and I. A. Richards of Harvard. To an old friend and former associate in administrative work, Arthur Calvert Smith, whose death in 1945 deprived Harvard of a valuable servant and loyal son, I owe an unusual debt: his encouragement of my interest in free education and my attempts to formulate the characteristics of American society in terms of fluidity and opportunity was determining in its influence.

Many other friends have lent a hand in this enterprise, especially with the publication of this volume, even reading the proof sheets and making last-minute suggestions of great value. I shall not embarrass them by giving their names, however, lest they be held responsible for certain points of view which may be considered controversial by some readers. My gratitude to all who have aided is most sincere, particularly to my wife whose day-to-day help has made this project a reality and to whom this book is dedicated.

JAMES BRYANT CONANT

July 7, 1948
Cambridge, Massachusetts

CONTENTS

EDUCATION IN A DIVIDED WORLD

AMERICA'S FITNESS TO SURVIVE

This book is about American education, particularly about our vast system of free elementary and secondary schools. The free tax-supported schools are the sinews of our society: they are the product of our special history, a concrete manifestation of our unique ideals, and the vehicle by which the American concept of democracy may be transmitted to our future citizens. The strength of this republic is therefore intimately connected with the success or failure of our system of public education.

Some such set of propositions is the thesis of this book. Their validity must be tested not in terms of abstract educational theory but with reference to the state of affairs in the United States in the late 1940's. [Arguments about education in the kind of world in which we now live must be preceded by arguments about the kind of nation we want to build.] The relation of the United States to other nations, the structure of American society, and blueprints for future domestic and foreign policy are not only highly relevant to a discussion of education but supply the basic premises.

As to the probable course of events in the international arena, I shall venture a forecast for a few decades in the second chapter. In essence it amounts to a forecast of an armed truce for some years to come. Eventually this truce may be converted into an enduring peace: given time and a demonstration of the vigorous response of the United States to the Soviet challenge, we may gradually reduce the warlike tensions. But the time may be long, and courage, patience, and unremitting efforts on our part will certainly be required. General W. J. Donovan, writing in May 1948, declares that he does not believe war with Russia to be inevitable. "Why should the Soviet Union run the risk and uncertainties of a shooting war," he writes, "when through the chaos of the present peace it can continue to acquire vast territory and an industrial potential? The issue of war or peace depends on our will to develop the physical and spiritual strength of our people as a democracy. Only with this strength can we achieve both the resolution and the reasonableness which are necessary to win a lasting peace. And if we want a true peace, we must meet that test." In short, our hopes rest on the ability of the United States to be the leading partner in a semi-global development of democracy as we Americans understand the meaning of the word.

What is American democracy? In part a fact, in part a dream, and the latter is as important as the former. Indeed, one of the characteristics of our culture is our need to talk about the future development of the nation: a group of questions is central to all discussions of America's fitness to survive. What sort of society do we wish to develop here in the United States? Is this society to be continuous with our past development and a reflection of our traditional aspirations? Or is it to represent a marked deviation? If the former, what are the basic ideals of American democracy, and how can we further their realization?

What sort of society do we want here in the United States in the next one hundred years? To do justice to this question one should write a volume, but in spite of the complexity of the details I believe we can sum up our typical American hopes and aspirations in a relatively few words and phrases. Our American ideals spring from the history of this nation; in part they represent the strivings of all free nations, in part they are the product of the unusual conditions of our development.

Our political creed was formulated in a revolutionary era which had been nourished by the writings of the eighteenth century. From this heritage comes our adherence to a form of representative government based on free elections, untrammeled discussion of political issues, universal suffrage. Our legal system is founded on the centuries of evolution of the doctrines of the common law; we consider the rights of the individual as of paramount importance. Trial by jury, the writ of habeas corpus are as essential to us as the air we breathe; likewise, the civil liberties, including religious freedom, embodied in the Bill of Rights. However much we may differ among ourselves in the inevitable cleavage between the right and left as to specific measures to be taken by governmental bodies (local, state, or Federal), we never cease to think of officials of the government as *our* agents. Conservatives and radicals alike join in repudiating the totalitarian notion that the State as such is a mystic entity to be worshiped or a transcending force to direct the lives of ourselves or of our children. All this is obvious but worth restating if only to contrast these political ideas common to all democracies with certain unique ideals which are the hallmarks of American democracy.

To my mind, these ideals which I shall sum up by the words "equality of opportunity" and "social democracy" are a product of our special history. In the first place, this nation unlike most others has not evolved from a state founded on a military conquest. As a consequence we have nowhere in our tradition the idea of an aristocracy descended from the conquerors and entitled to rule by right of birth. On the contrary, we have developed our greatness in a period in which a fluid society overran a rich and empty continent, and one of the highly significant ideals of the American nation has long been equality of opportunity. This implies on the one hand a relatively mobile social structure changing from generation to generation, and on the other, mutual respect between different vocational and economic groups; in short, a minimum of emphasis on class distinction. That is why we Americans so often refer to a man as being "democratic" when we have reference not to his partisan affiliations but to his social habits. That is why we Americans have insisted that our public schools be so far as possible ladders of opportunity.

As we are all coming to realize, in reviewing the past forty years, the impact of the European radical doctrines of the nineteenth century based on the notion of a class struggle confused the thinking of some of our reformers of the early days of this century. These foreign doctrines have to a considerable degree diverted the attention of forward-looking men and women from the social goals implicit in our native American tradition. As a consequence, we have thought too little of our system of public schools — the concrete expression of our belief in equality of opportunity — we have thought too little of this system of universal education as an instrument of national policy.

Our type of political, social, and economic system is on trial in the grim world of the mid-twentieth century. We must regard it as a growing, changing system moving gradually forward toward certain distinct and characteristic goals. These include:

1. The continuation of a form of government based on free elections and free expression of opinion.

2. A continuation of the many relatively independent government units, towns, cities, states, and the Federal government — a flexible though complex system which allows for the maximum of "home rule."

3. A much greater degree of honesty and efficiency in all these governmental units.

4. The continuation of our highly competitive economic system with its wide divergence of pecuniary rewards.

5. A greater degree of social mobility and fluidity and a lesser degree of social distinction between occupational groups.

6. A greater degree of equality of opportunity for the youth of each succeeding generation.

The last two ideas are typically American. They are the essence of the uniqueness of our concept of democracy. Neither political nor social privilege comes to one by right of birth according to our American ideals. On the contrary, the members of each new generation are supposed to start from scratch. Merit alone should win. Of course, the cynical may shrug their shoulders and say this is theory — the facts of modern American life are far different. Granted, but that leads immediately to the central issue — our fitness to survive.

Ideals in an open society like ours represent goals toward which men and women may move by concerted action. They never can be reached in practice — almost by definition — but we can readily recognize whether we are moving toward them or retreating. Our American ideals in part correspond to the aims of all democracies, in part they represent a special contribution to the world. If we are to survive we must make these ideals explicit by our actions; words alone will not suffice. It is essential that we continually and critically reassess the rate of progress: complacent acceptance of ideals will be of no avail; never-ending efforts must be made to move society forward.

To the degree that the American people are united in their definition of their objectives we can count on the solidarity of the nation. For the morale of a free nation no less than that of any group of men and women depends in large measure on agreement as to the ends for which all labor.

One of the highly significant ideals of the American nation has long been equality of opportunity. This concept may well represent an exportable commodity sorely needed by the other democracies of the world today. There is considerable reason to believe that the absence of this ideal in France and Italy, for example, has been responsible in no small measure for the inroads of communistic philosophy and the subsequent sympathy with Soviet foreign policy. To the degree that we can demonstrate in the next few years that this unique American doctrine is no mere myth or legend, we may both contribute to the stability of other nations and forward our own democracy along its historic path.

In short, we are committed as a nation to a set of ideals quite in opposition to a social structure rigid by virtue of hereditary place. We are committed to equality of opportunity as an ideal — a goal. We are likewise committed to an industrialized society with a high degree of competition. Our problem is to make these ideals operate as constructive social forces and to eliminate the anti-social aspects of the greedy side of competition. How this may be done by stressing a variety of social patterns and providing many social hierarchies will be the subject of later chapters.

Equality of opportunity means equal opportunity for the youth of each generation; the phrase as applied to adults has little or no meaning. Theoretically one could have a society in which practice was a close approximation to this pattern. But a moment's consideration makes it plain that there is a fundamental conflict between a general desire to give all children in a community an equal chance and the special desire of each parent to do the best he can for his own offspring. Even in Russia today, where we are told equality of opportunity for children is more nearly a fact than elsewhere, there must be the same conflict at work. How far are the leaders of the party, the managers of the large factories, the successful generals willing to forego any advantages for their children?

Wherever the institution of the family is still a powerful force, as it is in this country, surely *inequality* of opportunity is automatically, and often unconsciously, a basic principle of the nation; the more favored parents endeavor to obtain even greater favors for their children. Therefore, when we Americans proclaim an adherence to the doctrine of equality of opportunity, we face the necessity for a perpetual compromise. Now it seems to me important to recognize both the inevitable conflict and the continuing nature of the compromise.

The compromise is quite workable and there is wide latitude for moving farther in either direction, that is, away from or toward equality of opportunity. The present situation is not one of those in which any appreciable alteration destroys the nature of the balance. Quite the contrary. An examination of various localities shows that already in the United States there are wide variations. Instances of very restricted opportunity and instances of very wide opportunity for children of the lower income groups may be easily discovered. Those of us who argue for a far greater degree of equality would be satisfied, I presume, if in the coming twenty-five years the conditions throughout the United States were to be brought up to the level of the best that now exist.

Of course, there will be those who reject contemptuously any idea that we must base our educational philosophy on a compromise. They are too impatient to dwell in any halfway house. In practice these idealists tend to join hands with the cynics who declare that such phrases as "equality of educational opportunity" are obvious rubbish. "When you get right down to brass tacks," the hard-boiled critics say, "the goal you picture of an even break for all children in a given town or city, let alone a whole state, is so far removed from reality that it doesn't make sense to talk about it. Education at each grade, getting a job, fitting into the group are bound to depend primarily on the position of the father, so the less said about 'all men being created equal' the better, except on Fourth of July occasions."

This objection is worth dealing with both as a specific argument and as an illustration of a perplexing problem which we face as a democratic people; furthermore it influences profoundly our ethical education. If "noble sentiments" and "fine phrases" are in reality but aspirations which critical analysis shows can never be realized in practice (at least not in the framework specified), should they be "debunked" and discarded in the interest of honesty and effective thinking?

The ideal of equality of opportunity may be derided quite as easily by those who take their orders from Moscow as by those who are sympathetic to a stratified social system. To both, talk of equalizing opportunity in a country operating on the basis of private ownership and profit is just so many words devoid of meaning.

The critics from the two sides must be given different specific answers. But the most important answer is a general one, an answer which can be made to all who belittle the significance of those "noble sentiments" once enshrined in the creed of all American liberals. As long as a national ideal — be it equality before the law, personal liberty, social justice, or "in America there are no classes" — as long as an ideal represents a goal toward which a community of free men may move by concerted action, the phrase in question has real meaning. As long as one may say of two cities or two states that one is nearer the goal than the other, then

clearly the "noble sentiment" in question has both con-
creteness and relevance for the nation.

How near we come to the realization of equality of
opportunity at the present moment is a subject to be
considered later. But no matter how far we may be from
the realization of the ideal, the influence of this concept
on the development of the United States has certainly
been of great significance. In spite of slavery, of the
landed aristocracy of the South and the families of sea-
port merchant princes, in spite of later industrial barons
in the North and East, the ideology of the United States
has remained fixed in its rejection of the doctrine of
inherited privilege.

How powerful was the ideal of a classless nation —
classless in a unique American sense — is demonstrated
by the way in which the problem of the immigrant was
handled in the late nineteenth century. Unlike the newcomers of an earlier period, the immigrants of this time
settled not in the open spaces but in urbanized industrial centers. They arrived at a point in both time and
space where large sections of American society were
rapidly undergoing a social stratification. These new
aliens might have become a class apart, permanently
differentiated by their language and foreign culture,
and permanently assigned to an inferior economic
status. The fact that this did not occur is of prime
significance. But more important still are the under-
lying reasons why the American people repudiated such
a solution of their industrial problem.

A statesman of the sixteenth century, conversant with the history of the human race only to that time and suddenly dropped in the United States of 1900, might have asked some strange questions. He would have been particularly skeptical about the then current zeal for Americanization of the foreign-born. "The recent immigrants," he might have remarked, "came here of their own free will. Certain nationalities, relative newcomers to this continent, have taken humble positions in a great industrial pattern. Some must be the hewers of wood, the drawers of water. Why not let these foreign immigrants and their descendants play this role? Fate has solved for the United States the labor problem." Our visitor might have continued, "You did not have to conquer another nation and make the outlanders do your bidding — other nations have come to you for this very purpose. Do not 'Americanize' them; let them keep their own cultures, their own languages; it will be easier to place them in the social scale."

So might have argued publicly a cynical and worldly-wise visitor to the United States. Just what would have been his fate I am not prepared to say. At least tar-and-feathering. Such direct action by the mob would have illustrated one of the grim and unruly elements which are also part of the American heritage. But the significant fact is that this so-called "realistic" view would have shocked the majority of Americans in 1900. A point of view quite reasonable to many a social philosopher of other days would not have received a hearing in the United States at the turn of the century. For here it was accepted as an axiom that these newcomers — once they were naturalized — were citizens with full rights. Their children were as much Americans as the children of those families who had first crossed the ocean eight generations earlier. There was no question of establishing the descendants of one group in any one vocational level. Few would have dared breathe this idea openly.

Half-consciously we in the United States recognized that if our ideals were to be preserved in an industrial society it was more essential than at an earlier time to amalgamate completely these newer arrivals. A campaign of Americanization and of education sprang forward on all sides. The results of this unconscious decision on social policy will affect the future of this country for years to come. Already the once widely discussed problem of the "melting pot" is beginning to fade. The first World War and subsequent legislation diminished the flood of immigration. In the meantime, the process of amalgamation had begun to show results. In the 1940's the phrase runs "we are immigrants all." We recognize today that this nation of which we are citizens carries forward a cultural stream to which many nationalities and races have contributed a vital part.

The historians of some centuries hence, surveying the United States of the early twentieth century, may be inclined to ponder on the puzzle of this self-denying ordinance of those in power. Even today some may wonder why when the tide of immigration was flowing strong the older inhabitants strove to assimilate the newcomers on a basis of equality. Yet a failure to understand the answer is a failure to understand the true nature of our traditions. An ideal proved more powerful than self-interest of the moment; the doctrine of freedom and equality rode down the economic forces which were forming separate classes. The principle of no hereditary privileges still dominated the American dream.

"There are no classes in America." This phrase has been used countless times to emphasize our belief in equality of opportunity. It has never been more effectively used than by Garfield in his historic answer to Macaulay's famous prophecy of doom for the United States. The English historian had predicted in 1857 the eventual collapse of any nation which had universal suffrage.

It is quite plain [he wrote], that your government will never be able to restrain a distressed and discontented majority, for with you the majority is the government, and has the rich who are always a minority absolutely at its mercy.

General Garfield replied in 1873:

I venture the declaration that this opinion of Macaulay's is vulnerable on several grounds. It leaves out the great counterbalancing force of universal education. But furthermore, it is based upon a belief from which few if any British writers have been able to emancipate themselves; namely, the belief that mankind are born into permanent

classes, and that in the main they must live, work and die
in the fixed class or condition in which they are born. It
is hardly possible for a man reared in an aristocracy like
that of England to eliminate this conviction from his
mind. . . .

The English theory of national stability is, that there must
be a permanent class who shall hold in their own hands so
much of the wealth, the privilege, and the political power of
the kingdom, that they can compel the admiration and obedience of all other classes. . . . Where such permanent classes
exist, the conflict of which Macaulay speaks is inevitable.

One may remark parenthetically that today this is
sound doctrine in the Kremlin. Garfield and Macaulay
agree with Marx and Lenin in their estimate of the explosive force inherent in a stratified society. From
which it follows that to defeat the high hopes of the
believers in the Communist doctrine we must prevent
such stratification. But let Garfield draw his own conclusions.

We point to the fact [continued the Civil War general
later to be president] that in this country there are no classes
in the British sense of the word — no impassable barriers
of caste. Now that slavery is abolished we can truly say
that in our political society there run no fixed horizontal
strata above which none can pass. Our society resembles
rather the waves of the ocean, whose every drop may move
freely among its fellows, and may rise toward the light until
it flashes on the crest of the highest wave.

This belief of Garfield has been in one form or another as constant an element in our American idealism
as the more often quoted ideals of personal liberty and
representative government.

As further evidence on the same point one may quote the historian Frederick Jackson Turner:

> Western democracy through the whole of its earlier period tended to the production of a society of which the most distinctive fact was the freedom of the individual to rise under conditions of social mobility, and whose ambition was the liberty and well-being of the masses.

But this excursion into the past will seem worse than useless to some readers. It will appear as an attempt to draw the red herring of a pioneer civilization across the trail of "capitalism," the source of all evil in this mechanized world. This will be the prompt conclusion of all who follow the Marxist line. It will be self-evident to those who believe that only by the liquidation of private ownership can freedom and democracy be obtained in an industrialized society. A "classless society" in an American sense is a contradiction in terms, they would maintain. Strictly speaking, they are right. The word "class" is defined by the expositors of modern Marxism in terms of the ownership of the tools of production. Where you have private ownership you have by definition, they would argue, an owning class. But let it be noted carefully that "class," when used as a weapon in an argument by adherents of the Soviet view, almost always means a closed hereditary class. The evils of a caste system are always contrasted with the Utopias they paint.

This is no mere quarrel about words, but goes to the heart of the answer of the American past to the present

Russian challenge. According to the strict use of the word "class" by followers of Marx and Lenin, we in America are committed to a class society. But in the sense in which Garfield was using the word, to the degree that class implies caste, *we are not*. This distinction, which many of us feel to be of the utmost importance, we must remember is essentially nonexistent in European lands. In the view of a vast majority of the citizens of this country, equality of opportunity would have meaning only in a political democracy and could be realized only in a competitive society in which private ownership and the profit motive were accepted as basic principles. Our answer to the Soviet philosophy is peculiarly our own. If our reply can be made convincing, the new ideas of an immigrant society may finally seep back into the parent nations; but for the present we stand in an almost unique position.

It is "up to us" to keep our system not only operating but improving, and thereby refute the predictions of the followers of Marx and Lenin. Military defense is, of course, required in a period of an armed truce but the basic issue is our ability to go forward with our own development as a free people. As the former Secretary of War Henry L. Stimson has said, "We must make it wholly evident that a non-aggressive Russia will have nothing to fear from us. We must make it clear, too, that the western non-Communist world is going to survive in growing economic and political stability. If we can do this, then slowly — but perhaps less slowly than we now believe — the Russian leaders may either change their minds or lose their jobs. The problem of Russia is thus reduced to a question of our own fitness to survive."

If my diagnosis is correct, our fitness to survive in a divided world is related to the power inherent in our traditions. Our future national strength depends to a large measure on wise and intensive cultivation of those elements in our democratic culture which are peculiarly our own. At the same time the responsibilities of world leadership require us to extend the boundaries of our interest and our sympathy as never before. We must formulate the goals of our free society in terms consistent with our past, yet force our imagination to leap two oceans. For if we are to combat the Soviet philosophy on other continents, not only must the morale at home be high but our foreign policy must be farsighted and courageous. Surely we deserve to survive only if we prove worthy of the duties that the military defeat of the Axis powers has imposed upon us. There is no room for chauvinism, complacency, or isolationism in our thinking. We can be both intensely American and yet international-minded, both loyal to the unique manifestations of democracy in the United States and staunch friends of free societies of all types wherever they may be found. Indeed, one is tempted to go further and say not only is such dual loyalty a possibility, it is the essential condition for the freedom of this nation and the continuance of Western civilization.

2

THE WORLD DIVIDED

Our fitness to survive the Russian challenge clearly depends on many factors, but it depends primarily on a vigorous demonstration of the vitality of our own beliefs in democracy and freedom. I have already indicated what a key role education must play in such a demonstration; but before developing this theme further, a few words more are necessary about the nature of the Soviet philosophy which today divides the world.

But is it a fact that the Russians divide the world, a few readers may inquire? Indeed, is the world divided? Are we not witnessing merely a temporary period of high tension between former allies? If so, why emphasize the grim and depressing aspects of what must be but a passing phase in the history of the relations of two great nations? If the estrangement between the United States and the Soviet Union is indeed merely the inevitable disagreement between powerful nations recently united in a great war, then the objections are well taken. If, for example, the basic issues between the Kremlin and ourselves are essentially the same as those that existed between Russia and England after the Napoleonic wars, then foreign affairs could well be relegated to a secondary place in discussing our educational plans. As in so many matters in the year 1948, one's conclusions derive from one's analysis of what goes on beyond the alleged Iron Curtain.

How seriously should one take the present differences in ideology between the Soviet Union and ourselves? To answer this question one must appraise the evidence available as to how seriously the leaders of Russia take their own philosophy. One must have a diagnosis of the men who now rule so ruthlessly behind that Iron Curtain.

There are roughly three points of view current in the United States which in their extreme forms may be summarized as follows: there are those who think the dwellers in the Kremlin are Slavic followers of Thomas Jefferson and the enlightenment of the eighteenth century, or at worst the early socialists of the nineteenth century; that all their aggressive actions are based on fear of the capitalistic and imperialistic United States. The second viewpoint, the antithesis of the first, is expressed by those who feel that the rulers of Soviet Russia are equivalent to the men who once surrounded Hitler and Mussolini; that they are military gangsters planning to conquer the world by war. Or a variant of this theme is to believe that they are the military descendants of Peter the Great, bent on Russian expansion of a nationalistic sort by force of arms. The third position, to which I am inclined, lays far greater emphasis on the ideology of Soviet Russia and of the parties which follow the Soviet line. According to this view, the leaders of Soviet Russia and the governors of their satellite countries are fanatic supporters of a philosophy based on the writings of Marx, Engels, and Lenin. While military force would be used by the totalitarians whenever it was found advantageous, the chief reliance would be on the efficacy of their own doctrine. The very basis of the Soviet philosophy, let us remember, gives the comforting assurance that history is on their side. According to their view, in due course of time every other nation will undergo a revolution, and a dictatorship of the proletariat will be established; then eventually when a capitalistic encirclement has given place to a totalitarian socialistic encirclement throughout the world, the state will wither away. Thus the rulers of the totalitarian states envisage their Utopia, and they seem quite prepared to assist the course of history by keeping a steady pressure where they can.

Perhaps because I take the effect of education very seriously, I am convinced that the younger leaders of the Soviets will be even more doctrinaire in their thinking than the older men now in power. When one examines even superficially the kind of "general education" given at every level in the Soviet school and university system, one is impressed with the particular type of outlook that must be characteristic of the well-educated Russian now in his early thirties.

Unlike the Nazi and Fascist philosophy, the Soviet body of ideas has a long and fairly consistent history. Furthermore, one must freely admit, it has made converts, though not many, among well-educated men in other lands, men of high intelligence at least in specialized areas. I am thinking of certain of the British and French scientists. The writings of these men, as well as such books as John Somerville's *Soviet Philosophy* and the translations of Russian educational documents by Counts, should be read by those who tend to minimize the influence of ideology on Russian thinking. To my mind, Soviet philosophy is something neither to be laughed off nor to be treated as a vile obscenity; we cannot afford to pass it by in contemptuous silence.

In the free market of ideas I do not believe the Soviet doctrine can stand up for a moment against the devastating analysis of those who start from other points of view. Such a free market does not exist in the Soviet Union, however, nor do I believe it will for many decades. A free market of ideas assumes an educational system which believes in a free market and impresses this belief on children, let it be noted. If one can imagine a miracle and suppose that all adult thoughtful Russians overnight deserted the standard of Marx and rallied to the ideas of Lincoln, shall we say, there would still be the task of reëducating all the children and youth between five and twenty-five in a new philosophy.

There will be those who grant that there are fundamental and continuing differences between the Soviet doctrines and our own, but jump to the conclusion that Russia is set on a course of military conquest and that war is the only answer: they combine the second and third of the positions I have outlined. I believe this conclusion to be false, for it fails to give sufficient weight to the reliance of the Communists on the power of the ideological component of their thrust westward toward the Atlantic. I recognize that this is a highly debatable topic and that the experts disagree. There are those who emphasize the nationalistic quality of the Russian doctrine. To these analysts it is not Soviet philosophy but pan-Slavism which is dividing the world: to them Marxism is but a screen used by men who are emotionally concerned with the domination of Europe by the Slavs.

While everyone must admit that there is a strong element of nationalistic or pan-Slavic doctrine in the Soviet philosophy, it seems to me the ideological power derives from the international appeal of the Marx-Engels-Lenin dogma. Russian history and the Russian character cannot be ignored in any diagnosis of the troubles which divide the world; but does not the evidence indicate that it is the Russian version of Marxist doctrine which threatens to dominate Europe rather than Slavs in high positions backed by Russian troops? Marxism, to be sure, was given its twentieth-century form by Lenin who added the conspiratorial method of waging the class war; Soviet philosophy owes a debt to the Russian revolutionary tradition but it claims to be universal. One of the hopeful factors is the possibility of an eventual clash between the doctrinaire followers of the Soviet philosophy in non-Slavic nations and those who give the orders from Moscow, or of an increasing hostility of the totalitarian rulers of the Slavic satellite states toward "Mother Russia." We who believe that war is not the answer to the Russian ambitions must base our hopes on the eventual disintegration of the Iron Curtain. To assist this process every chance must be seized to penetrate into the totalitarian nations through trade and cultural interchanges.

Those who tend to minimize the significance of the official philosophy of modern Russia and emphasize the historic Russian drive towards Europe may be either hopeful of immediate peace by negotiation or advocates of extreme belligerency on the part of the United States. In whichever camp they are to be found, they will talk largely in military terms and old-fashioned strategic settlements. I believe them to be wrong. Not that I have any illusions as to the willingness of the Kremlin inhabitants to use force to hasten the inevitable day when totalitarian socialism becomes a reality on a world scale. But I doubt if the Russians propose to accomplish their ends *primarily* by military force. I do not imagine they dream of Slav Commissars controlling directly the Channel ports, but rather of trusty Dutch and Belgian Communists ruling in the name of the Benelux proletariat throughout the Low Countries. The Russian military might based on ground troops hidden behind the Iron Curtain is to my mind but a secondary component of the two-pronged offensive, the Communist ideology and the tight-knit political organizations which are its vehicles being the primary source of strength.

A story which I heard a year or so ago, while perhaps apocryphal, will symbolize the way I am inclined to think the Kremlin regards the future. An American newsman was talking to a member of the Soviet foreign office sometime in 1946 and the subject of atomic energy came up. The Russian is alleged to have remarked, "Of course, we don't really take the atomic bomb seriously here in Moscow. No one who understands the Marxist philosophy could take it seriously." This was too much of a conundrum for the American and he asked for a further explanation. "Oh," said the Soviet official, "every Marxist knows that the next war will be a civil war, and you don't use atomic bombs in a civil war." (The last statement, I might note parenthetically, I believe to be sound reasoning. A weapon of mass destruction which requires large targets is not a weapon for a civil war.) If Russian officials think largely in terms of the present Russian version of Marxist doctrine, then they would regard it as almost certain that the next war would be a civil war. Furthermore, they would be convinced that the eventual triumph of their point of view was assured. Nevertheless, they may be counted on to do the modern equivalent of "keeping their powder dry." We must do likewise. But a consideration of the subject of America's rearmament I postpone to the concluding chapter.

A great many consequences for the United States

flow from the analysis of the Russian attitude which I have outlined. I am here concerned only with the repercussions of a divided world on the future of our type of free society, and thus on our educational planning. I cannot refrain, however, from a footnote, so to speak, on the need for a vast amount of scholarly work to determine to what degree this or any other analysis may be correct. Without a better understanding of the way the Russian rulers think — "how they are wired," as one American delegate who argued daily with them has said — without a better knowledge of Soviet philosophy and an accurate estimate of its hold on individuals, we are shadow-boxing in many areas. For example, are the Soviet apologists simply lying in the grand Hitlerian style when they try to make us believe that a ruthless police state is a democratic country? Can they possibly be sincere when they talk of the freedom of the Russian citizen as being greater than our own? I think they are both sincere and lying, and this strange contradiction is basic. They are sincere in the belief that their type of organization alone gives freedom or points the way to freedom for the "masses"; lying when they resort to any verbal tricks to confuse the enemy, "the committees of the owners," "the ruling class" in the capitalistic nations. If this estimate be right, then the world is indeed divided and will remain so for a long, long time to come. That is why I believe a discussion of foreign affairs must precede an examination of our educational system.

Sincere and intelligent Russians and Americans are bound to regard the future in different terms for many years — in different nationalistic and in different ideological terms. Emotional words like "freedom," "democracy," even "truth" and "beauty" have entirely different overtones for the two groups. But since both are confident that their philosophy is "right" in both an absolute and a pragmatic sense, both should be willing to leave the matter to the peaceful unrolling of the scroll of history by the hand of fate. A global war is nonsense for both sides. The recognition of the danger of stumbling into such a war in which neither side can win ought to be a sufficient deterrent to prevent the holocaust.

I need not devote a single line to arguing against a so-called "preventive war." It is criminal folly to advocate that the United States should attack Soviet Russia, whichever of the three positions one takes about our former ally; it is particularly absurd for those who tend to the third position, which I think should be the basis of our planning. We must not be blind, however, to the twofold nature of the threat and the realities of the European situation. Unless we can balance the Russian military potential, our efforts to revive the economy of the sixteen nations under E.R.P. and thus repulse the ideological invasion will be in vain. Of course if the American people should be foolish enough to follow those leaders who would have us turn our backs on Europe, then either the triumph of Communism on a global scale or World War III would seem inevitable. But granted a certain degree of prudence and enlightenment on the part of the government of the United States, we should be able to avoid these harsh alternatives.

To some, the prospects for the future, indicated by the diagnosis of the present to which I incline, will seem too grim: decades of a divided world, the only two great industrial nations living in two separate "universes of discourse"? This is too horrible to contemplate, too unstable to endure. To others, it will seem too rosy, and my failure to equate the present rulers of Russia with international gangsterism or military imperialism will be written off as "soft-headed." The objections from the more optimistic or the more pessimistic usually add up to one word — war. If we make up our minds that a divided world is unendurable, or that the Soviets are either gangsters or military-minded aggressors, then war will come. But that it will be a solution of the problem, hardly any intelligent person can maintain. What would lie on the other side of a third world conflagration is perhaps idle to envisage. But assuming that we should conquer Russia, what would happen then? Can anyone imagine our occupying and policing that vast country for even a few months, let alone a period of years? Does anyone think the social, political, and economic problems Europe inherits from a feudal past, nationalistic rivalries and the industrial revolution will be made less formidable by a third World War? These questions should stop any advocates of an attack on Russia by the United States. A consideration of these same questions should make those who dislike the prospects of a divided world more reconciled to facing a future dominated by a long-drawn-out conflict between two opposing doctrines.

A competition between two points of view, reflecting two cultural patterns, may be resolved in the course of time without a military struggle. But the time needed is long; much patience is required. As both cultural patterns change, what once seemed issues of life and death may become adjusted within the new framework. Surely, one could document such a view of history from the religious wars following the Reformation, or even from the collision of the Mohammedan and the Christian worlds. It is perhaps fruitless to speculate on the ways in which the tensions of the present may be eased in the course of a few decades if a global war can be avoided. But the first requisite is surely the demonstration that there is in fact a strong and vigorous rival to the Soviet views. This demonstration must convince even the most doctrinaire followers of Marx and Lenin that at least their time scale must be wrong. One can hardly expect at the outset to do more than persuade the Soviet philosophers that the advent of world communism has been postponed. But once they are convinced that not within their lifetime, not indeed for generations, is the prophecy of Marx and Lenin to come true, the Russian rulers may proceed to negotiate in a very different spirit. From that point on, the nature of the competition between ourselves and the Soviet Union will alter radically. While the world will remain divided still, the possibility of some degree of confidence in the realm of sound negotiations will revive.

But what can convince the Soviet leaders, someone may ask? Not words but facts: the stubborn fact of the successful leadership of the United States among the non-communistic nations. This requires capable leaders of broad vision here at home, and a solidarity within the nation to back them up. Complete agreement about ways and means is, of course, an impossibility; our unity is based on a wide diversity of opinion on all sorts of matters. But the basic premise is a free competitive society which holds promise for the future to large numbers of the people. We must have not only prosperity but a movement forward consistent with our inherent idealism. We must every year move nearer our historic goals.

Granted private ownership and the profit motive (which have been sneered at in certain circles, but for which I believe there is no substitute for this nation), the question of how best to keep our society truly competitive and moving toward a greater degree of equality of opportunity is not easy to answer. I suppose few would really subscribe today to the old doctrine of "hands off." As in the case of traffic, the nature of modern society has made the public a party to what once seemed a strictly private matter. The role of government has been permanently enlarged. The political machinery of government is today meshed into our industrial life. The problem surely is to see how we can operate our private enterprises *and* our political institutions so that our society will be in fact competitive and thereby increasingly productive of the goods and services required.

Nor is it merely a question of economics and political organization. The factors of morale, of incentive, the fears and hopes of millions are all important. In this connection Mr. Francis, the Chairman of the General Foods Corporation, may be quoted: "To attain positive industrial peace, we need something more than by-laws and compulsory rules. We need productive teamwork. We need men working willingly together toward known goals. We need, in short: workers who are informed; workers who enjoy a sense of security; workers who are given a feeling of individual dignity; workers who are properly and fairly paid; workers who are given non-financial incentives." And in the same article, speaking of the self-analysis of top management, he asks the question, "Do we believe that political and economic freedom are inseparable, and that they are equally the rights of employers and employees? There is no literal warrant for this interpretation in the Constitution," he goes on to say, "but I happen to be one of those who believe that you can not put freedoms in separate compartments or maintain one kind of basic freedom without the other." Like so many other leaders in industry, this executive realizes that in the application of sound knowledge about human relations lies the possibility of answering some of the hardest problems we have to face in making our industrialized democracy work as a dynamic society of free men.

Few would deny today that economics, politics, and social ideals are thoroughly interwoven. People demand answers to the questions: "Where are we going?" and "If we know where we are heading, are we moving forward or losing ground?" The Soviet leaders readily supply answers to all their followers and supporters in every nation; in particular, one simple answer: "History is on our side."

There is no corresponding easy slogan for the citizens of a democracy with our traditions — no simplifying generality. Therefore, we have to consider a set of detailed questions and be specific and realistic in our replies. To do this we must be better students of human nature than were our predecessors in this century. The last thirty years have taught us that modern industry and trade do not proceed in a social vacuum and that human beings do not behave like economic symbols. We must analyze our problems not only as economic questions but in terms of human motives, of social ideals, and the relation of these ideals to a well-formed picture of the future of the nation.

This is increasingly admitted except in extreme radical or reactionary circles. For example, people are coming to realize that a discussion of taxation must involve more than a consideration of fiscal policy: it must in-

clude social ideals and the effect of taxes on human
motivation. High inheritance taxes reflect the American belief in a fluid society without a hereditary privileged class. We shall want to keep these taxes high
in order to insure that our American idea of a classless
society will stand firmly in opposition to the Soviet
challenge. Yet we realize the importance of the rewards
and incentives which actuate most Americans. These
are a complex mixture of social ideals and personal
aspirations including the desire to provide for one's
family after death. We shall not want our tax laws to
be so drastic as to block powerful human incentives
from having desirable social and economic consequences. The American public must consider the conflicting factors and strike a balance. High taxes on
earned incomes, it may be noted, have the reverse effect
of high inheritance taxes on the fluidity of our society.
In so far as the national expenditures permit, the case
for keeping income taxes low is overwhelming both in
terms of social ideals and incentives. The most important point, however, is a realization that social ideals
and human motives as well as balanced budgets and the
welfare of our national economy must be considered in
a formulation of our tax policy.

As never before, business needs executives who appreciate the responsibilities of business to itself and to
that unique society of free men which has been developed
on this continent. Such leaders must understand not only
the practical workings of business organizations but also

the economic and social climate in which business operates. Management and labor share with the statesmen whom we elect to office the responsibility for our future. Less directly, but ultimately to an equal degree, so do those who guide our vast system of public schools. They should be statesmen, too. Professional men and leaders of opinion, particularly the bar and the press, are likewise heavily involved. Cannot all these people, indeed the majority of our citizens, subscribe to a common set of postulates as to what we desire to accomplish in the coming years? The goals of equality of opportunity, a minimum of class distinction, "fair play for all," a maximum degree of individual freedom, and a wide distribution of centers of initiative are inherent in the American creed. If the United States is to continue as a vigorous and healthy republic of free men, it must continue to move toward these goals. Cannot we all, or a very large fraction of us at least, agree on that?

If so, then the first condition for national unity is assured. Our sights are set, our target is defined. But it is no easy matter to move appreciably toward these goals even if we are all agreed as to the direction in which to head. A modern technological society is a complex affair, and to find the correct answers to countless detailed questions puts heavy strains on man's intelligence and patience. The going will be tough, no one can gainsay that. Statesmanship will be required not only in affairs of state but in other vital areas; two in particular are of prime importance: industry and education. As to the first, almost every reader will agree; and the significance of the second is the thesis of this book. Their close connection, however, is not always realized — nor the need for solving problems in both areas by a coöperative approach. Yet one may reach such a conclusion from the following considerations.

The future prosperity of America depends on the capacity of its economy to remain dynamic while providing satisfying employment for all capable of employment. But every year some two or three million boys and girls mature and enter our society looking for jobs. We believe they are all entitled to a fair chance. Clearly our educational system must guide and educate such a diversity of talent for employment in industry as may best forward the interests of the whole nation. There are many facets to this interrelation of education and industrial employment, and the word "guide" in the preceding sentence is one that deserves heavy emphasis. But a discussion of these matters must be left to later chapters. Here I wish only to point out that it is obvious that the best minds of the country should be devoted to a study of the many problems arising as a consequence of our endeavors through industry and education to keep this nation prosperous, strong, and democratic.

The methods of certain of the social sciences have already been developed to a point where studies of society by competent scholars can provide basic informa-

tion to assist the leaders of the nation. The scholars in
these disciplines can help train not only public officials
but those who carry responsibility for resolving the many
human problems in our complex industrial economy. We
must expect no miracles, of course, but certain types of
work in sociology, anthropology, and social psychology
seem full of promise. If basic research is as adequately
supported in these fields as in physics and chemistry, in
a few decades we should be in possession of much social
knowledge. Even today the point of view of the younger
men in these fields, if coupled with practical experience
and infused with a zeal to move American society along
its historic road, may be peculiarly effective.

Many of the educational problems facing this country, as the following pages indicate, are to a considerable
degree sociological. Not a few of them would seem
ready for analysis by modern methods and should yield
to a concerted attack by those who are trained in the
fields to which I have just referred. Indeed, the next
few chapters are but a rough sketch by an untrained
observer of a vast area which is ready for exploration
and development by professional scientists. That such
men now exist, with many more being trained in our
universities, is one of the facts that leads to an optimistic
view as to the future of this nation. If public education
is as important as I believe for our success as a free
people, then in the "cold war" with the Soviet Union
the scientists who assist in improving our tax-supported
schools will play as significant a role as did certain physi-

cists and chemists in the battle against the Axis powers.

George M. Harrison, Chairman of the A. F. of L. Convention Committee on Education, wrote in January 1948 as follows:

Sometimes men build better than they know. A ship survives the buffeting of a typhoon and all aboard are saved. A lone building remains standing in Hiroshima after all else has been leveled by an atomic blast. So it is with education in our country.

The founding fathers of our nation conceived a government based on the consent of the governed; a government that exalted the individual citizen by giving him freedom, equality and dignity before the law and in the eyes of his fellow men. In a few short years they were followed by a few men of vision who saw clearly that these concepts required implementing by the understanding of the people. Thus, they proposed and succeeded in establishing a free educational system that has spread the length and breadth of our nation.

That educational system has reached into the minds of the great majority of Americans now living and instilled such a standard of individual freedom and dignity, and a belief in the government as the servant of the people that they will not fall easy victims to the propaganda of totalitarianism.

The confidence in public education thus expressed is typical of the attitude of forward-looking Americans throughout the land. Labor and management, professional men and women, in short, all the citizens of the country, must look increasingly to our free schools for the effective demonstration of our answer to totalitarian ideologies in a divided world.

3

EDUCATION AS A SOCIAL PROCESS

We sometimes fail to realize to what extent education underlies our whole economy; we likewise fail to understand how this fact affects the social structure of the nation. If the citizens of this country are to become increasingly active participants in providing better public schools they must become deeply interested in educational matters. This means a willingness to study the school and the community with a frank recognition of the complexities of modern life. Not as educational amateurs but as voters and taxpayers pledged to support and improve our free schools, people of every age should direct their attention to American education. If they do so, they will encounter some difficult but fascinating questions — problems which demand on the one hand a penetrating analysis of American life and on the other a clarification of our basic philosophy. The nature of these problems, and their relation to the future of our democracy are too little understood. Our approach to education is often far too personal.

The almost revolutionary change in the role of formal education in preparing men for fruitful participation in the national life has had far-reaching effects in this century. When education more advanced than the elementary schools was hardly required except for a few professions, a man might make a career for himself without benefit of formal learning. The fact that the few colleges in colonial America were inaccessible to poor boys of the eighteenth century made little or no difference. Even as late as the middle of the nineteenth century the study of law and medicine required as a prerequisite hardly more than a partial mastery of the three R's. The self-made man — the hero of many a true story of the United States of the last one hundred years — was a self-educated man. In business of all types including technical enterprises, in applied science (then in its infancy), in the traditional professions, a man not only could earn a living but could become a leader even if his schooling had ceased after the seventh grade.

Some seem to believe the same is true today. But such thinking is merely an example of a cultural lag. For the one man in a thousand who is a genius anything is possible, but otherwise it is perfectly apparent that even a man with great native ability whose education stops at the end of grammar school has many doors of opportunity firmly closed. The case is so obvious with regard to the professions (including science and engineering) as to require no demonstration. But let us consider for a moment what the effect of the increasing emphasis on the value of college training for a businessman has done to the social structure of the country. How many junior-executive positions in large industries are open for men now under thirty who have never been to any kind of college? From all the evidence I can gather, relatively few. What are the chances for a young man who broke off his education half way through high school to work up to a position of responsibility in a bank, a large merchandising establishment, or a far-flung industrial company? Remember, he is in competition with graduates of colleges, technical schools, and universities. Of course, cases will occur to prove the old saying that you can't keep a good man down, but what I am trying to underline is the contrast with the industrial picture of the 1870's.

If we examine the methods of waging war, the marked differences between conditions today and a century ago are brought clearly to a focus. For the mode of warfare reflects the general cultural pattern of a civilization. Modern battles on land, in the air, and on the sea require an incredible complexity of machinery; this machinery must be designed, produced, kept in repair, and operated. To do this requires a vast number of trained men. Comparing the mobilization of the man power of the country for World War II with that of France or Germany for the Franco-Prussian War of 1870 is like comparing the Battle of Gettysburg with Agincourt.

In an era when so many highly trained men are required for war, at least a corresponding number must be available for peace. At the time of the Civil War, the Army and Navy required very few officers and men who had more education than the ability to read and write. Indeed, both sides could and did make effective use of many who could do neither. The great expansion of the country after the Civil War likewise depended but little on the services of what we would now call educated men. But the future of the next few decades will be far otherwise; the role of trained men in a peacetime economy will become predominant. The contrast between 1870 and 1950 will be as great as that between the armies of Grant and Lee and those of Eisenhower and MacArthur.

From such considerations it is clear as crystal that in those cases where the kind and length of education to which a boy or girl is entitled depends on the accident of birth, the subsequent career is likewise largely so determined. In short, to the extent that educational opportunity is determined by geography or by family status, the increased importance of formal education in modern America tends to make for social stratification.

One should hasten to add that along with the revolutionary change in the significance of education in the preparation of young men for life in industry and commerce has gone an equally revolutionary spread of public education. The one has made for the hardening of class lines, the other has worked in the opposite direction. Where the balance lies no one can say with any certainty. It would be my own guess that so far the sum total effect of all the changes in American life since the 1870's has been to increase the stratification of American society. This I think is true the country over, except for the immigrants of the late nineteenth century and their descendants.

But whether or not I am right about this is a matter of no consequence. What concerns us is the future. Our present widespread system of education holds within itself forces which can move us either toward or away from our goal of equal opportunity for all children. We would be well advised, therefore, to debate the issue freely. If the American people want a more fluid society, we must plan our education accordingly.

Let us look at some of the facts. When we do so we shall see that as a nation we are indeed a long, long way from anything like equality of educational opportunity. Furthermore, we shall see that conditions vary enormously from locality to locality. And the more we study the matter the more complex the picture seems. Not only parental pride already mentioned and economic inequalities now much in the public eye, but cultural patterns, religious forces, and group hostilities must be reckoned with if we are to move further in the direction of reducing inequalities of education. Social prejudices and deep-seated tensions involving race, color, and creed will be met in more than one locality.

First, as to certain over-all statistics: before the war, of every 1000 pupils enrolled in the fifth grade, 770 entered high school but only 417 graduated; 146 entered college, of whom approximately a half completed their college course. These figures present the average picture for the entire United States. In some states a larger proportion of the students of college age would be found attending college; in others, a far smaller number.

Anyone familiar with education knows that for a very considerable portion of the population it is the family financial status which places a ceiling on the educational ambitions of even the brilliant youth. The oft-repeated statement in certain smug circles that "any boy who has what it takes can get all the education he wants in the U.S.A." just is not so; it is contrary to the facts. After having made that flat-footed statement, let me hasten to insert the comment that compared with any other large nation, except possibly Russia, we might appear to be living in an educational paradise. But measured in absolute, not relative, terms the discrepancy between our ideal and the reality becomes so great as to be almost shocking.

The figures of Warner and Havighurst in *Who Shall Be Educated?* give us a picture of the social stratification in a midwestern city before the war. The percentage of superior high school graduates who attended college followed the parental income scale in a startling manner, starting with a 100 per cent college attendance for those whose family income was over $8000 a year, dropping to 44 per cent for the range from $3000 to $2000, and falling to 20 per cent for those with incomes under $500. These were all superior students, let us bear in mind; all, therefore, good college material.

There is no need to give a mass of figures to show that a large number of talented youths in different parts of the country drop out of high school or fail to enter college because of lack of funds. Educators who know the situation conservatively estimate that as many promising boys and girls fail to go to college for economic reasons as the number who now enter.

In no place in the entire country can we claim to have come very near the goal of equality through education, but in certain of our large prosperous urban areas we have come a long way indeed. In these localities the statement is very nearly true that no brilliant pupil — that is, brilliant as measured by orthodox academic standards — with ambition can fail, because of a financial handicap, to get the education he wants.

If we think of the educational ladder solely in terms of scholastic ability (aptitude for "book learning"), then in certain of our large cities careers are freely open to the talented within the framework of our present social mores. This is so because the high schools are adequate for the boy or girl who does conventional studies easily and because first-rate universities which a student can attend while he lives at home are located in these cities. And the cost of going to college is, of course, only in small part the cost of tuition and student fees. Room and board and the increased expenditure for clothes to keep up with the academic "Joneses" mean a relatively large outlay for a youth from a poor family. There is also the possibility of part-time employment being greater in large urban areas than in smaller centers of population As a consequence, working one's way through college in a city involves not too heavy a handicap. All of these favorable statements are made with the reservation that I am leaving out of account the important and explosive problem of racial and religious discrimination.

The opportunity for advanced education (professional education, in particular) at low cost, which is afforded in a number of large cities, is in part the result of the accidents of location of privately controlled universities or state universities, in part the result of municipal action. It is interesting that however much the pattern varies in detail for historic reasons, the end result is the same almost without exception. Very few cities with a population of more than 600,000 are without a university with high standards, granting professional degrees including that of Doctor of Philosophy.

I estimate that somewhat less than one-fourth of the male white population between the ages of ten and sixteen now lives in urban areas within convenient commuting distance of a satisfactory university. We may rejoice at the fact that for such a considerable portion of the population conditions are so favorable for the white boy of intellectual promise irrespective of family income. There is another side to the picture, however. In the competition for that leadership which depends on a combination of innate ability and lengthy education, the youth of small cities, towns, and rural areas are at a considerable disadvantage. When we look over the enrollment figures for the dozen or so largest universities and know to what extent the student body of many is recruited locally, we realize what a large portion of university enrollment comes from urban areas. We have a very lopsided representation of the nation. This is reflected in the professions. And, of course, in business the cards are stacked even more in favor of the city boy from a low income group as compared to the corresponding boy from a town or village. This one-sided recruitment of our professions and executive groups from the cities is a social phenomenon of considerable significance. We see here at work a process of geographic stratification.

The suburban high schools of the country are the pride of our public school system; they are part of the urban education to which I have just referred. Here taxes are usually sufficient to support public education generously, and in the well-to-do localities a homogeneity of population makes the task relatively easy. In fact these excellent schools, together with the private schools, are potent factors tending to crystallize our social order. This is worth pointing out. It is as much an accident of birth that one's family lives in a prosperous residential district which affords an excellent high school (particularly excellent when judged as a preparatory school for college) as it is that one's family can afford to send one away to boarding school. In short, all high schools do not automatically make for national equality of opportunity.

Much of the discussion among laymen about the public schools tacitly assumes that education is purely an intellectual process. There is much talk about the value of this philosophy of education or that, of the need for emphasis of one subject as compared with another. But there is little realization of the great variety of problems facing our public schools and insufficient analysis of the sociological phenomena taking place within any given school. Not only laymen but some educators (particularly those connected with higher education) often look at the schools from an abstract point of view. Indeed, the head of one private preparatory school once said to me that the ambition of every high school outside of the rural areas was to emulate the good private schools! This man who had spent his whole life in school work admitted he was unaware of the fact that in many large cities there were high schools where less than 15 per cent of the graduates went on for further education. Clearly such a school operates in an entirely different social setting from the suburban high school cited in the preceding paragraph.

Some figures from New York State are illuminating on this point: for every 1000 pupils enrolled in the fifth grade in New York's public schools in 1931–32, 505 graduated from high school in 1938–39; 132 entered institutions of collegiate grade the following year. As contrasted with these average figures for the entire state, which show 26 per cent of the high school graduates going on for post-high school education, the percentages for single cities varied from a low of 12 per cent to a high of 57 per cent.

To laymen who pass judgment on the public schools one cannot repeat too often: education is a social process, our schools and colleges neither operate in empty space nor serve identical communities. Before you judge a school, analyze the families from which it draws its students and the opportunities presented to its graduates. What may be a satisfactory curriculum for one group of pupils may be highly unsuitable for another. And the difference is often due not to discrepancies in the intellectual capacities of the students but to the social situation in which the boys and girls are placed. This in turn depends on the nature of the local community of which the pupils and their parents are a part. To be specific, the problems facing the principals of three high schools — one in an industrialized section of a congested steel town, another in a rural area in the Middle West, a third in a well-to-do suburb of Chicago, St. Louis, or New York — are totally different. In the first two cases, for example, only a very small fraction of the graduates of the schools will expect to continue formal education; in the third instance practically all the pupils and their parents will expect the schools to prepare them for admittance to a college or university.

Such facts are so obvious when stated as hardly to warrant being recorded. Those who have spent their lives wrestling with the problems of public education are so aware of them as to take them for granted. Yet until recently many who were dealing only with college students talked about school problems as though such facts were nonexistent, or at least of no relevance to the educator. This attitude has been reflected in some of the discussions in what are sometimes referred to as "intellectual circles." In general, it implies the belief that a young person's mind is a sort of blank tablet on which the educator may write. If we can only find "good teachers" and the "right" education for them to impart, every boy and girl will be developed into a perfect citizen of this republic by the formal educational process. This is hardly an exaggeration of the attitude of certain writers.

The proponents of this view, being themselves "intellectuals," have in their minds for the most part an intellectual Utopia as the goal of any nation. Their discussion of schools and colleges rests on their own set of values, including their own professional aims. Everyone is to be a teacher, a scientist, a writer, an artist, or a highly literate statesman, lawyer, doctor, or possibly an engineer. To the extent that industry and agriculture are operated by a variety of workers, the future envisaged is one where the hours of work are few and those of leisure many. In these hours of leisure the libraries, museums, and concert halls will be filled to overflowing. In short, the avocations of the American people will gradually approximate the vocational interests of those who now earn their living as masters of one or another of the media of communication (including teaching) or as scientists or scholars.

As those who have patience to read this book to the

end will discover, I am not one to disparage the values inherent in a life dedicated to study and teaching or to the creation and dissemination of works of art. But the inadequacy of the outlook of the average intellectual when face to face with the realities of the United States is nowhere more tragically reflected than in certain recent books and articles about education. The nature of these inadequacies Granville Hicks has depicted in a forthright manner in his excellent little volume entitled *Small Town*. Depending on the degree of humanitarian idealism which is coupled with the outlook of the type of intellectual I have in mind, one finds either a negative Toryism or a radical utopianism as the social philosophy providing the basis of the debate. There is apt to be implicit in the discussion of schools and colleges either the feeling that really only the education of the leaders matters (the leaders being defined in intellectual terms) or that a rapid change in our social order will make everyone or nearly everyone an ardent devotee of the "life of the mind," at least in his or her spare time! The somewhat dubious and far distant prospects that atomic energy may revolutionize industry have been exploited by this group who talk in terms of an age of leisure.

It scarcely needs saying that the approach to educational problems put forward in this book is quite different from the one described in the preceding paragraph. Without being "anti-intellectual" it attempts to treat of education in terms of the present diverse motivations of different kinds of people. Without being defeatist it is far from being visionary. If, as I believe, we need to turn loose a group of young social scientists to study our educational system, it is important to agree as to what should be studied. Is it not the total social situation in a community? Matters of educational philosophy, curricula content, pedagogic methods are subordinate in such an inquiry. What come first are all the questions which highlight the fact that education is a social process. For example, the investigators of a given educational situation must ask all sorts of questions about human relations among students and their families; they must also seek information about the unwritten conventions and customs that determine to a large degree the behavior of individuals.

My straw man or woman, bluestocking critic of the public schools, should be ready at this point to raise strenuous objections. This is the relativistic and materialistic approach run wild, he or she should hasten to assert; quite irrespective of the social setting of a school, education should be concerned with the wisdom of the ages and its orientation determined by a series of absolute values! Is there to be no attempt to *change* the behavior of human beings through education; is there no role for the teacher in elevating the standards of judgment?

My reply would be that I contend it is possible to combine the analytic approach of the sociologist or anthropologist with a firm belief in standards. I think it is not inconsistent with American idealism to recognize the barriers that block the road to our Utopias.

The point of view that I should wish to see pervade our public schools would be that of a tough-minded idealist; on the one side it leans heavily on a certain type of social science, on the other it is almost fanatically humanitarian, tolerant, and individualistic. Without being chauvinistic it gains strength by its close connection with the indigenous stream of American idealism. Indeed, there must be enough of this American idealism in the mixture to insure against any disguised Toryism's gaining the upper hand; there ought to be enough tough-minded critical quality also to prevent the planning of Utopias from usurping all the energies of our educators.

The only working hypothesis for Americans, it seems to me, is a belief that by the collective use of our intelligence and a mobilization of our good intentions we can mold the history of the next fifty years within certain limits. To speculate beyond fifty years is an interesting but unprofitable undertaking. That philosophies which purport to understand "the laws of history" and prophesy the future have done much damage to our free society scarcely needs to be argued in the face of the advance of Marxism in Europe.

The working hypothesis just proposed is not to be confused with the belief in progress so characteristic of liberal theological writing in America and England before World War I. No evidence appears to be at hand for any trend in the universe toward a goal where human misery is less than in the past or the sum total of human happiness is greater. In fact, one may question whether on critical analysis such phrases have real content. Progress in techniques and skills and certain types of knowledge has been enormous over the centuries. But the relation between accumulated knowledge and skills on the one hand and human satisfactions or lack of satisfactions (suffering) on the other is very complicated and uncertain. In short, I see no need for believing that we are living in a world which automatically is getting better and better; there is no evidence that we are on a roller-coaster where one can relax and think of the inevitable goal of sweetness and light that lies ahead. Instead, it would appear that modern man can be sure only that tragedy has always been, and for centuries to come is likely to be, a constant aspect of the human drama. *But not the only aspect.* Good fortune and disaster go hand in hand. Collectively, in the last few decades we Americans seem to have had far more than our share of luck.

At all events, we are in a position to guide our destiny more nearly by our own efforts than most societies in the past or at the present moment. But first we must be sure that we understand and appraise correctly the current scene; then we must have in mind our future goals. If we accept the premise that education is a social process, there need be no apology for the next chapter of this book, which deals with the structure of American society.

4

THE STRUCTURE OF AMERICAN SOCIETY

At times radicals speak as though a human society were possible without diversification of employment and without concentration of responsibility and authority in a relatively few people; that is, without a structure. When they do, they are apt to be challenged sharply by conservatives. They are reminded that a society as structureless as a town meeting probably has never existed for any length of time, and the probability that an industrialized society could run without a hierarchy of authority seems small indeed. But the conservatives may then proceed to a totally unwarranted assumption: namely, that the present methods of determining who shall serve in the various positions of a complex social order are the only methods which could possibly exist. Since obviously some must rule, why all this talk about "privileged group" and "ruling class," the conservatives may demand.

Both radical and conservative are apt to miss an important point. Practically every society — a nation, a town, a city, a rural area — has at any given moment a fairly definite social structure. But this may vary greatly in a number of important characteristics which in the last analysis count heavily. Even in the final phase of Communism, when the state has "withered away," society must have an organization, for industry will not run without a high degree of diversification of labor. Indeed, I think the Communist doctrine is very vulnerable at this point; but that is another story.

Among the characteristics of a social structure we may note: (1) the complexity; (2) the visibility of group differences; (3) the mobility within the structure; and (4) the rate of change of the structure. Let me consider these points in order. If the relation of the individual to other individuals is determined by one social pattern, we have a simple social structure — a soldier in an army is a favorite illustration. On the other hand, if an individual occupies a position in several patterns simultaneously in existence, he is part of a complex social structure. For example, if a man is a skilled worker, the employee of a large concern, a member of a union, an important dignitary in a fraternal order, the natural leader of his immediate neighbors for political purposes, we should have to place him not in one social pattern, as in the case of the soldier in time of war, but in at least half a dozen. And since most social patterns tend to have an explicit top and bottom, we may speak of his position in each. To the extent that it may be high in one and low in another the complexities increase and the whole situation may defy description. The nearer we approach to such a situation, the less an individual is aware of the existence of a social structure; or in popular language the farther we are removed from a caste system. In many an American locality in the past, at least, this has been very nearly the situation.

Let us turn now to a brief consideration of the second way of characterizing a society, namely, in terms of the visibility of group differences. During the war we were all conscious of that mammoth social organization known as the army. Consider for a moment the social structure of the American Army on the day of Germany's surrender in 1945, and compare it with that of the Prussian Army in 1914. At first sight the two organizations might seem almost identical; both had a relatively simple structure in the sense that the position of each individual was essentially unambiguous; in both, the high visibility of the group differences was consciously rendered visible by outward signs. Yet let us examine the matter more closely, for we all have a feeling, based on countless bits of evidence, that the American Army was a relatively democratic one while the Prussian part of the German Army in 1914 was the epitome of militarism.

In the first place, the two armies differed in the higher echelons in regard to the degree of fluidity of the social structure. The Prussian officers represented a military caste very largely perpetuated from father to son; our American officers are, as one said to me the other day, "drawn each generation from the people." This point we shall return to later.

In the second place, in spite of the fact that both armies wore clearly marked uniforms and operated through the well-known chain of command, the visibility of group differences in the Prussian Army Corps of 1914 was much greater than that in the corresponding units of the American Army of 1945. At every turn the regimented nature of the Prussian Army was impressed upon the individual member. He was to have no life outside the life as a unit in one rigid social pattern. Our modern American Army, however, tried to keep the soldier aware of his own individuality as far as was consistent with military effectiveness; those social pressures were fostered which minimized rather than maximized the significance of the military organization. To be sure, the very fact that this was a temporary assignment for a vast majority of both officers and men set the scene. But, in addition, the Army apparently deliberately fostered a climate of opinion which "played down" rather than glorified a man's position in the hierarchy. Emphasis on performance irrespective of rank, recognition of the fact that each soldier was above all else a citizen of a free country, minimizing the privileges of rank, were some of the obvious steps to be taken to produce a democratic and individualistic army. That there was a considerable effort in this direction can hardly be denied even by those bitter critics who maintain that many further steps could have been and should have been taken. At all events, the American Army in Europe in 1944 was a relatively democratic organization.

I have drawn the contrast between the Prussian and

American armies in order to illustrate, first, that two social structures superficially similar may in fact differ to a considerable degree; second, that a simple structure may be modified considerably by consciously created social pressures and artificially cultivated modes of behavior — in short, both by action and by talk.

This point seems to me of considerable importance. Those of us who believe it is possible to move each generation toward a classless society in the American sense can take hope from this example. Note that one might have said: an army is by definition a simple social structure; every man in it must know his place and act all the time in conformity with that place; a democratic army is a contradiction in terms; a private who is an individual is an absurdity. But experience has shown that this kind of "inevitable" conclusion drawn from an oversimplified statement of a social situation is superficial and inexact. *Without changing essentially the organization of the army, it was possible to modify to a surprising degree at least one important characteristic of its structure.*

An industrial civilization cannot be maintained without a diversification of employment and a hierarchy of grades *superficially* somewhat analogous to an army. But there is a whole range of possible complexities of the resulting social organization; there is a similar spread of possible degrees of the visibility of the differentiations between groups. Indeed, as already pointed out, the greater the complexity the less the visibility.

Another important point is the fluidity of the social situation — the social mobility referred to in earlier chapters. If the top jobs are based on hereditary privilege and the bottom ranks are based on hereditary lack of privilege, if all the social pressures emphasize a man's position in this industrial hierarchy and assess a man's worth solely in terms of his rank and finally prevent other social patterns from developing, then you have something not unlike the Prussian Army. You approximate a caste system for the nation. The converse is obvious.

Fluidity within the social structure, changing status from generation to generation, complexity of the social pattern, low visibility of the group differences — all these are desirable if we would have an industrial society composed of individuals who regard themselves as free. And again, if over a period of years in any locality the social mobility and complexity increases and the visibility decreases, the rate of change of the social structure itself is high; indeed, I would maintain that a rapidly changing pattern of this type would, from the point of view of the individual concerned, closely approximate a society without a structure. That is to say, the men and women of each new generation would be faced with such different social patterns that to them it would seem as if they were living in something approaching a society without classes. During the rapid expansion of some of the urban centers of the Middle and Far West within the last century this was approximately true for large segments of the population. Because of this, the American ideals, about which so much was said in the first chapter, took form and shape and became strong elements in our tradition. How to achieve similar ends in the twentieth century seems to be the central question in the effort to organize a free society.

Frankly, I must admit that by no means everyone would agree with this; there are advantages in a caste system, though few would so state in public meeting. A society where everyone knows his place and operates willingly and efficiently in the place determined for him by the accident of birth has some very appealing features. As a utopian goal it attracts those who dislike the competitive spirit and all the unlovely aspects of human nature that so often accompany that spirit. As an acceptable utopian goal today, however, a high standard of living in even the lowest grade of the organization must be guaranteed. A socialistic picture can be drawn without difficulty in some such terms. But with a few changes in emphasis we transform the scene into a more familiar historical example where those in the lower levels, at least, did not consider their living standard high at all. And who is to be the judge of the distribution of luxuries and leisure as between the different layers? If one abolishes competition, the problem of rewards and incentives in a *free* society becomes increasingly difficult to solve.

How important it is to get these matters straight in our minds before we talk about public education is clear at a single glance. If we repudiate the ideal of a fluid social structure and wish to have the reverse, a stratified system of society, we must arrange our education accordingly. We should then provide from the elementary schools onward an entirely different type of education for each group of children, depending on their family background and in accord with the inherited position they will occupy when they grow up. We should inculcate not only obedience to authority but reverence for the hierarchical system as a system; we should stimulate each individual to get his enduring satisfactions out of his proper performance of the duties which by birth have come to him, and will in turn be the duty and the privilege of his heirs. The competitive spirit at every turn should be frowned upon and in its place the teacher must endeavor to show the joy which comes to one who has mastered the art of living the "good life" at his or her appointed level.

This is only a slight exaggeration of the spirit which has pervaded the development of universal education in Germany in the last hundred years and, to some degree, in other European nations also, even Great Britain. Much more is involved here, let it be noted, than the extent to which the schools are ladders of opportunity for all. What we are concerned with at this point is the way in which the educational system of a nation reflects the degree of "class consciousness" of the country. If we use the word "democratic" in the sense of being unconcerned with or oblivious to social differentiations (as it is so often used), then we may say that our American system of public schools is uniquely democratic.

To illustrate this point, let me take pre-Nazi Germany as an example. Germany had universal education for children long before the United States did. Germany also had excellent secondary schools and universities. At first sight you might say that as of the 1920's both nations were approaching closely to the goal of universal education. Yet the German educational system and that of the United States in reality were miles apart — almost at opposite poles; the difference reflected in turn the difference in the social structure and the social ideals of the two nations. Let me make it plain, I am not talking about Nazism; that nasty aberration of a highly educated nation is another story. The basic educational system of Germany was little modified by the totalitarian regime, though it was seized and used for propaganda purposes. The fundamental structure of the German schools today as in previous years reflects a stratified social order.

Let me quote from the report of an educational mission to the United States zone of occupied Germany in 1946. Speaking of the need for the development of the idea of the school as a primary agency for the democratization of Germany, the commission says:

This concept has not inspired the schools in the past [and the entire past is meant, not just the period of Nazi rule]. Very nearly, in fact at the end of the fourth year, the school has heretofore been a dual system, one for the five or ten per cent of intellectually, socially and economically favored who go on to secondary school, university and the professions; the other for the great group who have four years more of tuition-free elementary school and three or more years of vocational training. When he is ten years of age or younger, a child finds himself grouped or classified by factors over which he has no control; such grouping to determine almost inevitably his status throughout life. This system has cultivated attitudes of superiority in one small group and inferiority in the majority of the members of German society, making possible the submission and lack of self-determination upon which authoritarian leadership has thrived.

Now I think it fair to say that the system our educational mission found in Germany today is not unrepresentative of the basic educational philosophy of all European nations in the last one hundred years; yes, and even of that of our British friends, at least until very recently. To the extent that the few per cent who go up the educational ladder are chosen solely on intellectual grounds, the system can be considered democratic; to the extent that scholarships are available, careers may be said to be open to the talented. And in Great Britain the really brilliant boy — that is, brilliant in orthodox academic terms — has often had better scholarship opportunities than his opposite number in this country. That is why some of my British colleagues maintain that their educational system is far more democratic than our own. But even if the scholarship provisions were as generous as sometimes claimed, the system reflects a fundamentally different way of looking at society from that of the average American. Or, to put it the other way round, the American system of public education represents a unique type of universal public education. It is unique first, because there is little or no differentiation among pupils in terms of subsequent vocations till after the high school years are past; second, because a very high percentage of our youth finishes high school and a considerable percentage goes on for still further education.

The relation between the structure of our society and our educational system is reciprocal, of course. Our kind of universal education is one of the most powerful forces in reducing the visibility and increasing the complexity of our society as well as maintaining a high rate of social mobility. But we pay a price. To many well-educated and liberal-minded foreigners our system makes no sense at all. "Mass education, which ruins the talented," they complain — "education thrown away on vast numbers of the uneducatable," they often say. These well-meaning and highly-civilized critics, with their background of a foreign country and a stratified social system, completely miss the significance of what we are trying to accomplish in this country. Perhaps at times many native Americans also fail in this regard. For there is no doubt that the use of our public schools consciously or unconsciously to keep our society "democratic" and fluid presents us with an educational dilemma. The more we try to employ the instrument of universal education to offset those forces of social stratification inherent in family life, the more we jeopardize the training of certain types of individuals. In particular, we tend to overlook the especially gifted youth. We neither find him early enough, nor guide him properly, nor educate him adequately in our high schools.

Indeed, the criticisms now leveled against our public secondary schools from professional men are directed to this fact. The quarrel between our universities and our high schools stems from this fundamental dilemma. (And if a layman really wishes to hear eloquent evidence as to the inadequacies of our public secondary schools, let him talk to the professors on almost any campus!) There is no doubt about it, there is an inherent difficulty in our desire on the one hand to give a general education on a democratic basis for *all* American youth, and on the other, to give the best specialized professional training for a certain selected few. The dilemma is not insoluble, but it is important to recognize its existence — particularly so for non-educators, as otherwise much of the criticism of our schools is apt to miss the target. I hope to show in subsequent chapters how the two educational aims of our society may be reconciled to some degree. But at this point I should like to reiterate my belief that there must be no retreat from the emphasis on a flexible and democratic system of free schools.

In this brief analysis of American society as it pertains to education I have left to the last the most difficult and unpleasant subject — racial and religious prejudice and intolerance. While group antagonisms based on cultural differences made visible by personal characteristics occur in different forms in many areas in the United States, there are two particularly distressing problems. One is the future role of our Negro population. The other can be summed up by the word anti-Semitism. As Gunnar Myrdal has pointed out in his classic work on the first subject, our national idealism and our social practice are in head-on collision in these areas. This is the first point to be freely admitted. The second that needs emphasis is that in competition with the Soviet philosophy our present social mores on these matters are perhaps the most vulnerable spots in our armor. That being the case, we are going to hear a great deal about our shortcomings from sources which are by no means committed to forwarding the American traditions. But that does not mean we should sit back and do nothing about the Negro problem or anti-Semitism. Nor does it mean we should proclaim our ultimate goals as being attainable within a lifetime. It is worse than useless to attempt to banish social situations by noble phrases.

This matter of abolishing social hostility and intolerance is clearly an instance where we must recognize ideals as goals. We must demonstrate real progress every year but cannot expect to attain the ultimate objective. To achieve even this minimum the help of the younger social scientists is needed badly. In no area are tough-minded idealists, well trained in certain of the social sciences, more likely to forward the public welfare by their labors. We need careful studies and well drawn plans rather than broad pronouncements. For example, those of us who happen to have little or no prejudice in regard to the color of a man's skin are perhaps too prone to make a virtue of our particular tolerance. We may not assist the over-all progress by castigating the intolerance in other sections of the country. Sectional hostility is quite as real a social phenomenon as racial intolerance; the cure for the latter hardly seems to lie in increasing the former. Every thoughtful American citizen, whatever his personal prejudices, who believes in the American ideals which I have ventured to call unique, must work for a greater degree of tolerance between cultural groups. He must likewise work toward a greater degree of educational opportunity for those groups which are held back because of racial prejudice in various sections of the nation. These efforts must go hand in hand with attempts to modify industrial practice and the public reaction. No one but a utopian or a revolutionist can sincerely hope for a change of public opinion overnight.

If one accepts some such set of limited objectives, then clearly each city or town or state presents a special problem. Negro education in the South is one problem, in Detroit another, in New England a third. Combating anti-Semitism is equally a matter of geography.

That the country would be a great deal better off if careers were freely open to all the talented seems hardly a matter for debate. That our belief in a society with the minimum of class distinction is contradicted every time we segregate Negroes or discriminate against those of Mexican, Japanese, or Jewish ancestry is obvious. Recognizing always that education is a social process, the educator and the layman who wish to forward our American traditions in this divided world will work together in each locality. They will wish to reduce each decade the degree of intolerance and prejudice based on ancestry and to increase the opportunities for any groups where such prejudice is a handicap to education and employment.

5

GENERAL EDUCATION: THE HUMANITIES

Having considered an analysis of the structure of American society and the fact that education is a social process, we are now in a position to discuss certain broad issues hotly debated among teachers and administrators. We may approach these controversial matters by attempting to answer the simple question: Why should one be taxed to provide schools for other people's children?

The justification for spending public funds on a system of free schools in the United States, I take it, is threefold: in the first place, we wish to insure a vigorous development of this society in accordance with our traditional goals; in the second, we desire that as many of our citizens as possible may lead fruitful and satisfying lives; thirdly, we realize that in order to prosper as a highly industrialized nation we must find and educate all varieties of talent and guide that talent into the proper channels of employment.

The first objective may be designated as education for citizenship; the second as education for the good life; the third as vocational education of which professional education is a special case. I am using these phrases loosely; this threefold division of education may serve as a rough guide to a layman seeking to penetrate the tangle of verbosities which surrounds many discussions of the content of the curricula of schools and colleges. As a matter of convenience, we usually employ the term "general education" to signify all those aspects of formal training which contribute to the attainment of the first and second objectives. General education thus defined is to be contrasted with specialized education; the latter is directed toward the acquiring of certain skills and information and the formation of certain attitudes useful in a vocation. The separation of general education from professional education in our universities has led the former to be designated "liberal education." Today the term "general education" is used more frequently.

While this use of the two terms "general education" and "specialized education" (of which the subcategories are vocational and professional education) is useful, it is important to realize that in practice they cannot be sharply separated. In the elementary and secondary schools the fusion of the two elements should be as complete as possible. Overemphasis on the distinction jeopardizes the democratic nature of public education. There is also a danger that any logical analysis of education with terms carefully defined tends to obscure the fact that education is a social process; in this case, quarrels among educators immediately appear. To a large degree these quarrels (which reflect enormous difficulties in planning curricula) result from a failure to think about the educational process in terms of the social structure of the community which the school in question serves.

For example, I believe that an impartial analyst from another country listening to the discussions in various groups about "vocational training" versus "liberal education" would come to the conclusion that the chief point of disagreement was not the content of education, but for whom the education was being planned. Take a group of public school teachers who year after year have been dealing with high school pupils from a congested area. Listen to their discussion of "education for citizenship" and then compare their premises as well as their conclusions with those of a gathering of professors talking about "liberal education." One has difficulty in finding a common denominator for the two discussions, though in purely formal terms both are concerned with the general education of American youth.

I am inclined to think our ideal of a nation without classes checks to some extent a frank treatment of the educational problems of the country. We instinctively shrink from using phrases which imply that there is one type of education for the well-to-do, another for the poor. Perhaps having an uneasy conscience as regards the discrepancy between the realities of American life and our proclaimed ideals, we tend to avoid an analysis of educational problems in sociological terms. Educational discussions usually proceed as though education for a future citizen of the United States, now aged fourteen, were totally unrelated to his home, relatives, and friends. Yet we know that a school drawing a vast majority of its pupils from the lower income groups in an urban area does not have the same problems as an expensive private boarding school. To deny this is equivalent to denying the existence of the force of gravity.

If we started our discussions more often by an analysis of the particular community served by a school, we should make more progress, both toward understanding our problems and toward developing public education as an instrument for shaping American society. We must admit, however, we are traversing a dangerous and narrow ledge whenever we seek to deal candidly with the problems of society. And this is not because of the animosities which would be created by a public dissection of a given city or town. Rather, it is because we want our schools to be forces to obliterate or at least soften social differentiation. If we had all the teaching fraternity analyzing their day-to-day problems in terms of the structure of the portion of American society they serve, we would be forwarding the very thing we wish to avoid, namely, increasing the visibility of the social pattern. Indeed, one might argue that discreet silence on all such matters, coupled with the bland assumption that all Americans *have* equal opportunity, is the way to forward American democracy; any other procedure would stir up class feeling and play into the hands of those who want to perpetuate a caste system.

Though admitting the extreme difficulties involved

in probing into such delicate affairs, I am convinced that a fuller discussion of the present social differentiation in American life is essential. But it should be in terms of either a specific situation or a classification of various types of situations. Furthermore, the undesirable overtones of such a discussion will be softened to the extent that we can rid ourselves of an adherence to one hierarchy of social values. The book-reading public and those who write for it place at the apex of the one and only social pyramid a high standard of competence in literary and philosophic subjects. As a consequence, this group has been by and large unduly critical of the public schools, and for the reasons indicated in a preceding chapter.

But much more is involved than praise or criticism of modern high school curricula. The fundamental issue is to what extent we wish to equate the old world ideal of a "learned scholar and a cultured gentleman" with the goal of our general education. If we regard the schools and colleges which shape their practices to this end as being vastly superior to all others, we are perpetuating the old notion of an inevitable separation between the "educated" and the masses. To the extent that we can achieve a greater equality of social status between individuals with a variety of educational backgrounds, we have moved into another educational world. In so doing, we have repudiated the nineteenth-century notion that it requires "three generations to educate a gentleman."

There is a fundamental issue here. One sees it coming to the surface most frequently when colleges are discussed, but in reality this issue is the crucial point in connection with planning secondary education. To be sure, educators beat around the bush for the most part rather than lay bare the central proposition. We have great hesitancy for the reasons just referred to in facing up to the social implications of general education in the kind of country in which we live; we are reluctant to expose to the light of public debate those obvious differences in our educational procedures which are related to the social and economic status of the families from which the children come. We want neither to emphasize the fact that these differences exist today nor to admit that in terms of occupational ambitions similar differences are part of our cultural pattern. Yet if we do not analyze the situation in terms of the social structure of America today, we can neither plan our education wisely nor move in the direction of a minimizing of class distinctions.

Roughly speaking, the basic argument about general education turns on the degree to which the literary and philosophical traditions of the western world, as interpreted by scholars and connoisseurs before World War I, should be the basis of the education of *all* American youth. The watershed between two fundamentally opposed positions can be located by raising the question: For what purpose do we have a system of public education? If the answer is to develop effective citizens of a free democratic country, then we seem to be facing in one direction. If the answer is to develop the student's rational powers and immerse him in the stream of our cultural heritage, then we appear to be facing in the opposite direction. By and large, the first position represents the modern approach to education; the latter the more conventional view. Those who look down one valley regard conventional "book learning" as only one element in the landscape; those who look down the other believe that developing the "life of the mind" is the primary aim of civilization and this can be accomplished only by steeping youth in our literary and philosophical heritage.

Readers of the recent books on education will recognize not only the two opposing points of view but several variants of each. And since there is no sign that the debate is subsiding, it would be well for every citizen who is interested in improving our public schools to be aware of the arguments presented. What is involved here is nothing less than the role of the humanities in the fluid democratic society of a heavily industrialized nation. Conflicting views will be found when plans are discussed for general education at every level — elementary and secondary schools, colleges and adult education.

At the risk of oversimplifying a complex matter, I am going to present my own view in terms of an analysis of the place that the humanities should occupy in the kind of democratic society envisaged in this book. To do this one must talk in terms not of school programs or even college courses but of the continuing education of every thoughtful citizen irrespective of his or her vocation. For it is obvious that a general education is something that should continue throughout one's active life.

First, a brief digression on the use of the word "humanism" and "the humanities" may not be out of place. Cogent arguments can be presented for a number of different definitions, almost all of them flattering in one way or another to those who prize the labels. For example, in the academic world, there have been scholars who insisted that "humanism" was a term embracing all the activities of creative artists and learned men — scientists, historians, philologists, archaeologists, philosophers. From the professor's point of view, there are social advantages in such an all-inclusive use of a word with such pleasant overtones. For example, a scientist who has been fortunate enough to marry a poet and whose children follow the maternal bent may well desire to raise his standing in the family circle by proclaiming that he is in fact a humanist. Perhaps such verbal magic has its uses in this day when all creative workers are perforce specialists who none the less yearn for a common emotional basis for their work. Recognizing that "man does not live by bread alone," one may characterize the labor of artists, poets, scientists, and scholars by declaring that the sum total of their effort is the new humanism of our day.

There are grave difficulties in such attempts at

achieving unity even within a university, however. If all professors are by definition humanists, and all poets and artists also, and all preachers and learned divines as well, what indeed that is human is not part of the humanities? Only the vicious and the abnormal. But in this case the word "humanism" and its close relative "humanities" describe so much that they have ceased to be of much utility.

A narrower definition of the humanities seems to me essential if the term is to be helpful in discussions of modern education. I therefore am restricting my use of the word to the study of art and literature. My analysis will be concerned primarily with the art and literature of the past, but we need not define the past so arbitrarily as to exclude the past decades of this century. One can justify this terminology by an appeal both to history and to modern convenience. The first humanists were the scholars, artists, and writers of the Italian cities and towns who in the fourteenth, fifteenth, and early sixteenth centuries recaptured the art and literature of Greece and Rome. Since they transmitted a knowledge of the writers and artists of the past, one is not entirely departing from historic usage by limiting the word "humanist" to scholars and teachers concerned with one aspect of man's activities.

If this be true, humanism in origin had a dual nature. It was compounded of the fruits of intellectual adventure on the one hand, and aesthetic and philosophic insight on the other — the zest of digging and the joy of contemplation of the treasure found. This twofold aspect of the humanities persists to the present day and is a source of both strength and weakness. One may note parenthetically that the dual nature must be kept in balance. If the zeal for digging or its equivalent in philological terms becomes overriding, a type of desiccated scholarship results which has been the subject of attack now for many years. If the joy of contemplation of the beautiful becomes dominant, a sentimental attachment to some one period of literary or artistic taste is almost certain to result. The dynamic quality of true humanism disappears as the collector merely rearranges and admires those objects on which he has set his heart.

The teacher of the humanities today has the special task of rediscovering and transmitting a knowledge of man's activity as a poet and artist. The humanist today, as he was five centuries ago, is not only a discoverer but an interpreter and above all a teacher, whether his pupils be children, young men and women, or adults. In this task he will need as a constant ally the creative artist whose advanced training lies beyond the province of this book. I may only note that unless society encourages and generously supports contemporary artists, composers, and writers, there will be little sustained enthusiasm for studying the heritage of the past.

For those who have followed the argument of the preceding chapters, I need hardly point out that the humanist today, as always, must relate his work to the current social and cultural scene. Likewise I need not emphasize the fact that the social setting of maturing youths as well as grown men and women is vastly different in this country in the postwar period from anything the world has ever seen before. And if our plans for moving nearer our historic American goals are successful, we shall each decade move farther away from the cultural presuppositions of the Victorian Age.

In no place in the educational process does the revolutionary nature of this change of scene have more effect than in the teaching of the humanities. As a consequence, no phase of school and college, no aspect of adult education is at one and the same time more uncertain or more challenging.

The humanist for the last four or five centuries has had the task of transmitting a knowledge of and appreciation for literature and works of art. He formed the taste, or at least was a potent factor in forming the taste of "those who knew." Yet in every country where he has been successful his influence has reached only a very small fraction of the population. For only those with wealth and leisure were in a position to listen to his words. His pupils were sons of the hereditary aristocracy (in fact, if not in name) or those who aspired to become their social equals. His allies were men of position and wealth who collected libraries and works of art. His formal connection with educational institutions dates from the time when in a given country a university training became the hallmark of a gentleman. Perhaps this is an oversimplification, for I am ignoring the relation between the humanists and the theologians. But even this alliance, which first brought the humanists to the English universities, was nevertheless powerfully supported by the interest in the humanities of a few persons of high social status.

As a consequence of the connection between a leisure class and the humanities, a great element of snobbery was early introduced into the difficult matter of aesthetic judgment. For one "lover of the arts and letters," who had his own set of standards based on an informed appreciation and a natural aesthetic sense, there were ten collectors who had merely memorized the current "gilded dogma." This dogma changed somewhat but not too rapidly from generation to generation. It must change, of course, for otherwise there would be no pleasure in being up-to-date, no reproach possible to one's parents and friends who are so old-fashioned in their tastes!

I recite this obvious connection between the snobbery inherent in any leisure class and the arts and letters, not to belittle what men of wealth and position have done to advance civilization, but to throw a spotlight on the difficult problems of the present. In the year 1948, the leisure class is distinctly out of fashion. Rereading now Veblen's classic exposition of the "doctrine of conspicuous waste" (the alleged hallmark of the leisure class) is like watching a flight of swift arrows directed toward a target which has disappeared. With inheritance taxes at their present levels, universal educa-

tion through the eighteenth year now in sight, the all
but disappearance of a white servant class, and the high
geographic mobility of the young, we are living in a
society sufficiently fluid already to make it necessary to
reëxamine certain bench marks of our culture. Certainly no small group of youths in each generation can
any longer be counted on to be the arbiters of taste or
the allies of the humanist in his work as a transmitter of
cultural knowledge. This being the case, what is the
task of the humanist as an educator?

That he is in a difficult position is clear whatever
side one takes in the debate about the future; it is as
though a country parson who was used to ministering
to a small and homogeneous congregation should suddenly find himself assigned the task of being the spiritual leader of the crowd that fills the Grand Central
Station the day before the Fourth. I may exaggerate,
but if one compares the educational problems involved,
for example, in teaching English to the present body of
high school students in a low-income urban area with
the simple task of a tutor to the English nobility in the
eighteenth century, I think my analogy may not be
entirely out of place.

Some would say this is the century of the so-called
common man in education as in all other matters: let
the humanities be reformed to meet his needs. I dislike,
however, that way of putting it. Rather, I would say
that this is the century in which "we the people" have
come of age; and, coming of age, "we the people" re-

quire a maturing education. What have the humanists to give, and what are the functions of the humanists in this day?

Some have urged the need for adult education in the humanities as a means of preventing the boredom which is alleged to be our lot as a result of shorter working days. This argument seems to me far from convincing. I think the proponents underestimate the joys of leisure in the U.S.A. To many, the seats in the baseball grandstand still look far more attractive than those in the reading room of the library. And you can no longer entice pupils of any age with appeal to the higher snobbery. For if we can all have the knowledge for the asking, its snob value is very small. So "we the people" say to the humanists, you will have to "sell us" on the value of your understanding and appreciation of the past before we will even enter your classrooms, your museums, or your libraries. The social and parental pressures that once brought you humanists your well-clothed and well-born pupils no longer hold.

Sensitive souls who love art and literature but despair of democracy have been hearing some such taunts and jeers from the multitude for several decades. Call them barbaric cries, if you will. They are heard none the less. The question is, what should be the humanists' response? Hardly a voice is raised today to suggest that they should fight a rear-guard action, drawing around themselves the fast disappearing remnants of a leisure class. Rather it is widely accepted that they should revolutionize their educational concept and go out to meet the howling mob. How to do it — there is the rub.

Before the humanist gets down to details of curricula and pedagogic methods he has to answer the basic question: Why do the future citizens of this republic need to be exposed to the arts and literature of the past? To answer this the humanist must ruthlessly reëxamine the nature of his premises and seek new allies in this age of the machine and common man. He must muster his arguments to show the importance to the individual and to society of what he has to teach; and these arguments must be stated in such direct terms as to persuade the school board of an average American town. Why Shakespeare rather than the comic strips? It is usual to speak of the "empty trash" on which the average American feeds his mind. Why not, the skeptic may remark — what is the harm? Let the humanist not shudder at this barbaric question, but face up to it and answer it. Granted that it is his educational mission, among others, to teach men "to see, to hear, and to read," he must first persuade them of the need for real vision and a disciplined power to comprehend.

Not being a humanist myself, I should be pressing my competence far beyond the danger point if I attempted to answer in detail these distressing questions which "we the people" raise. Nevertheless, I suggest that by relating their educational undertaking to ethics, the welfare of the body politic, and the emotional stability of the individual, humanists can make an overwhelming case for the importance of their mission. The study of literature is a means by which a man may live a rich life; it may so "accumulate years to him as though he had lived even from the beginning of time." Surely it is easy to convince anyone of the wisdom that comes from a long life lived with understanding. Good literature can compensate to some degree for the limits which time and space put on each individual's knowledge of human nature. In order to achieve his or her place in the sort of society here envisaged, each adult should be as free from frustration as possible. We can hope to neutralize the emotional strains of a mechanized civilization by cultivating enduring satisfactions. And for many men and women continued acquaintance with literature and the fine arts provides just such satisfactions.

The heyday of private collectors and connoisseurs may well be over; perhaps only in so far as art is a form of personal experience will it have meaning for modern man. Certainly this is the best working hypothesis to accept in planning the introduction of art into school programs. It is so accepted in relation both to music and the graphic arts by those who are the leaders in modern schools. The use of the creative arts in public education, particularly at the primary level, as a technique for emotional release, seems to have proved its value. Great possibilities lie ahead for the expansion of this type of personal experience with art at every level.

To my mind, there is only one thing certain: the humanists must have courage and imagination as never before. Once the character of the changed scene is recognized, the vastness of the opportunities are apparent. As in the days when he first began to uncover the glories of the ancient world, the humanist stands at the beginning of an exciting and expanding era. He must rapidly increase his numbers with recruits of high caliber and arm them with the proper weapons. These weapons, moreover, must be chosen with the nature of the target clearly before his mind. There is no general prescription for the way in which art, music and literature should be presented to *all* American youth or *all* members of the adult community. For no one can assume a homogeneous audience.

To the degree that any given high school is a cross section of the social and economic stratification of the country, the study of literature will have to be presented with a variety of motivating forces. So too, of course, will the social studies and science, but the problem there is far less complicated. General education to such a heterogeneous body of students should be presented in terms of a wide spectrum of occupational goals. A school in which 90 per cent of the children come from families who hold a union card or are eligible to do so is one thing; a school in a well-to-do residential suburb is quite another. In the first case it is only the exceptional boy or girl who expects to enter a profession and therefore looks forward to a long period of further "schooling." The boy with ambition to succeed in the practical world will normally find his outlet by getting a job as soon as the high school years are done. Truck driving, for example, will be an opening for those who enjoy speed and that feeling of power that comes from handling modern machinery. In the second school, conditions will be reversed. It will be the exceptions who do *not* plan to continue education beyond high school; it will be the unusual boy who does not expect either to be a professional man or to enter industrial life via a white-collar job. Anyone seriously considering truck driving as a career would be looked upon as very queer indeed.

Now, to assume that the way the two schools teach literature and art should be the same is like assuming that the diet of a lumberman in the north woods should be the same as that of a desk worker in a southern city!

One cannot help having the feeling that different descriptions of general education at the high school stage are the result of focusing attention on different types of public schools, or, what amounts to the same thing, focusing attention on different types of students. And here we face again the educational dilemma inherent in our American system of which I wrote in the preceding chapter. If we direct attention to the final occupation of the student, we can more readily agree on the details of the general education at every level. But because we have a democratic and flexible school system, we are very anxious to avoid differentiation until after the high school years are passed. Even the separation

of the student body of one school into "college preparatory" groups and vocational groups has unfortunate
consequences if there is no common ground. The visibility of our social structure begins to increase at once.
For this reason the forward-looking educators directly
concerned with our secondary schools have attempted
to formulate a "common core" of learning suitable for
all the students.

While laymen have every right to examine such attempts at democratic unification with a critical eye, they
should be careful not to view the matter entirely from
the point of view of their own occupations. Take the
study of literature and history for example. To the
extent we are concerned with the education of that portion of American youth that comes from the upper
income group, or is extremely gifted in terms of academic
studies, we are perhaps justified in presenting those
subjects in what might be called an old-fashioned way.
The social forces at work on these young men, arising
from their background, together with vocational motivation, provide sufficient pressure to insure the temporary
absorption of a considerable amount of orthodox "book
learning."

The tradition of the learned professions, combined
with the emphasis on the significance of literature and
philosophical studies in the homes of the well-to-do, set
the stage for this type of education in this country
several generations ago. By the end of the nineteenth
century it became accepted that a boy who was either

going to enter a profession or be a business executive should have what was then called a "literary education." Parents, with few exceptions, understood this; a majority of the boys concerned understood it. As long as advanced education was concerned only with this group, the orthodox approach had relatively smooth sailing. As long as the high schools were essentially college preparatory schools, the real problems of general education so apparent today were hidden below the surface. Only when large numbers of youths with other occupational aims began to take part in high school education and go even further, was it necessary to probe more deeply into what are the basic aims of general education. When we carry out a more searching analysis of general education for *all* American youth (instead of merely one small segment of young men), we find that the study of the humanities must be approached from a revolutionary point of view.

Both the nature of the presentation and the reasons for the inclusion of the subjects in the school program vary according to the outlook of the student in terms of his or her ambition. This becomes evident by the time high school has been reached. For example, making a case for as thorough a study of literature as time permits by the future doctor, lawyer, business executive, or public servant is as easy as making a case for the study of mathematics by the future engineer. The arguments are not the general ones referred to earlier which are applicable to all citizens. Rather they are directed to the subsequent career of the student. Quite apart from his professional knowledge of law and medicine, the lawyer or doctor needs to be wise in his understanding of human beings; he will be concerned to a very large degree with relations — complicated relations — between highly sophisticated individuals. Wide personal experience with many varieties of people, particularly emotional experience shared in common covering the whole range of human joy and misery, provides at present probably the best preparation that is possible. The public servant who comes up through the give-and-take of the political arena and has sensitive human perceptions acquires his education in this way. As a substitute and as a supplement, the dramas, novels, and poems of the great writers provide a most valuable vicarious experience.

The situation is very different, however, when you come to consider either advanced education for a profession which is little concerned with complex human situations, or education for those who are to be concerned with running machines or with the distribution of the products of machines, or who are to work with their hands on the farm or at the bench. In such cases, I doubt if occupational reasons for the study of literature can be adduced which will stand the acid of youthful skepticism. Why should the future truck driver, shoe salesman, bank teller, or assembly line foreman read the English classics? Or, for that matter, why should the future astronomer, protozoologist, or research chemist? There is not a shred of evidence to indicate that a wide acquaintance with Elizabethan drama, for example, will make a man either a better astronomer or a better assembly line foreman; and it is folly, I believe, to argue that it would. The reasons advanced to the prospective members of those vocations should be in terms of *general* education. But not only the reasons but the pedagogic approach must be altered. The appeal must be to the students as future citizens.

No argument should be needed to convince the members of a high school class that they are all going to live in a closely connected, highly industrialized world which contains a vast amount of specialized knowledge. As citizens they are going to bump up against a complex variety of experience no matter how they earn their livelihood. Only on an isolated farm in a backward part of the country can any of them enjoy the simple life of their grandparents, who were quite content with a very small amount of "book learning." "To be ignorant of what occurred before you were born is to be always a child"; this was never truer than in this century. To be ignorant of the way in which the present technological civilization came to be is not only to live in perpetual bewilderment, but to be at the mercy of every man who claims to be giving you reasons why this and that are so. Now it is easy to show that literature is part of the history of the race. It is one record — a record no less significant because it is written in emotional rather than rational terms — of our cultural ancestors, a record which appeals by its very nature to all manner of people. This story of our past must be read in order to enable us to appreciate the present. Here it seems to me is the significance of the dramas, novels, and poems of the English-speaking people of the last three hundred years for the vast majority of our young people.

All concerned with the future of the humanities in the schools might well proclaim the fact that, since we are living in a technical and scientific age, some attempt must be made to relate the present of this bewildering scene to the much more simple past, else the whole picture becomes merely a series of magic shows. So, to the academically slow-minded youth who wants to do something practical, the appeal of the printed word must be an appeal to a story of simple origins in order to illuminate an amazing picture. Technological history, social history, a simplified account of certain philosophical ideas, political history, and the literature of each age are all related. Curiosity is more widely distributed than innate love of literature. Curiosity may be the basic motivation, therefore, to bring out in the vast mass of our pupils the willingness to immerse themselves in our cultural heritage.

The equivalent of the social pressure of the ruling class tradition that once made many a reluctant youth study the classics may be at hand in the evident bewilderment of so many people about the nature of the society in which we live. By appealing to the curiosity of *all* youth about the origins of an obviously complex and unintelligible technological society, we may evoke a willingness to learn about the past. But the nourishment which is provided to satisfy this curiosity must be really relevant to the present scene. No traditional arguments as to content will suffice. By different paths, different types of youth may be led to read and read voluntarily for pleasure and illumination. To the extent that our schools succeed in this, the horizons of our citizens will be broadened; they will be wiser and more stable as individuals; they will be less susceptible to the calls of modern medicine men who like to take advantage of the bewilderment of the average man in the presence of machines he does not understand; our general education in the humanities will be in tune with modern times.

6

GENERAL EDUCATION: THE STUDY OF MAN

In the last chapter we were concerned with the study of the art and literature of the past and present. The question was raised as to how the "leisure class" notions of what constituted an educated gentleman could be transformed into ideas applicable to the United States today. An analysis was attempted of the current disagreement about the degree to which a study of our cultural heritage should form the basis of a general education. I now propose to jump to an equally controversial topic, the study of man. The issues involved may be brought to a focus by suggesting two alternative titles for this educational area. Should one use the phrase "The Nature and Destiny of Man" or "The Behavior of Man as a Social Animal"? Should one of the two main currents of general education be described as an attempt to answer the question: "What is man that Thou art mindful of him?" Or should we rather say that the modern educational problem is to teach children how to grow up to live normal lives, which means "acquiring the proper responses to the batteries of social stimuli which compose our social order"?

For the moment, let me indulge in academic jargon; the subjects under discussion here are ethics, political science, economics, psychology, sociology, and anthro-

pology. History is the academic discipline which together with philosophy should form the connecting link
between these subjects and the humanities.

I have left theology off the list. This omission at once
leads us to the center of an ancient battle. Yet it would
be my contention that in so far as *public* education is
under discussion, we must leave out theology. Only a
completely secular school system can be supported by
the taxpayers and operated by our democracy. Otherwise, a public instrument will be torn asunder in the
conflict between rival theologies. This was well understood by the founders of this republic. They lived near
enough to the period of the religious wars to realize the
potential dynamite in religious controversy. Bishop
Laud and Cromwell were familiar figures in their minds.
To the extent that we have made a beginning in revising
this policy in the last few decades, a serious error has
been made. One may hope that the recent decisions of
the Supreme Court point to an interpretation of the
First and Fourteenth Amendments which will block any
further advance (or I should say retreat) in this direction. At the same time one may trust that no anti-reli-
gious fanatics will attempt to police our schools and
purge all references to religion. It would be absurd to
bar the use of hymns in connection with choral singing.

I recognize that this insistence on the separation of
secular education and religious education is completely
unacceptable to some people. A not inconsiderable number of those who are offended by the modern approach

to education are deeply religious persons who believe the whole concept of secular education to be bad. Not that all members of organized religious groups nor all people with intense religious feeling belong in this category. The vast majority of Americans of all creeds, I believe, feel that public secular education is not only possible but highly desirable and in no way inconsistent with the active work of the churches in stimulating the interest of young boys and girls. For them, as for me, there seems no other basis on which a nation of so many creeds can be united in planning for public education. But the minority who resolutely refuse to agree to a separation of education into secular and religious parts are often to be found in the camp of those who advocate the study of literature, philosophy, and history in the terms of a mid-Victorian Oxford don. They are likewise to be found among those who regard with suspicion the infiltration of the modern sciences of man into the academic world.

The question is repeatedly raised by the opponents of secular education: Is the secularization of education not the equivalent of accepting a purely scientific materialism as the national philosophy? The answer, I believe, is an emphatic no. Our public schools and our secular private institutions are not to be used as outposts for the propaganda warfare of *any* theological pressure group; and that includes those who crusade under the banner "All theology is meaningless." Furthermore, every shade of religious opinion in the United States, including no opinion, must accept the historical basis of our culture.

There can be no doubt that the Hebraic-Christian tradition with its emphasis on the sanctity of each human soul was one of the mainsprings of the development of democracy in this land of pioneers. This point has been made so often since the outbreak of World War II and documented so carefully that there is no need to reargue the case. There is further no doubt that it was militant Protestantism which by and large made this tradition the basis for American democracy. But neither of these facts requires us to use our public schools as advance bases for an attack on any one of the forms of Catholicism or the many varieties of agnosticism or materialism. Where the study of philosophy borders on theology, all that is required of the teacher is the presentation of the fact that within our culture there are many variants of one single ancient religious tradition; that in foreign lands there are other vastly different theologies and cultures which to some degree are likewise represented here.

We are a nation of recent immigrants. This fact must be kept in the foreground of any discussion of cultural and spiritual cohesion. In terms of world history we are all of us, except the descendants of the Indians, relative newcomers to the area we now designate the United States. We or our immediate ancestors carried across the ocean a variety of cultures, traditions and religious faiths. A wide diversity of beliefs and the tolerance of this diversity have constituted the bedrock of our national unity. They must continue to be the foundation for the peaceful growth of this republic.

Adopting this view, I believe it is possible for men of many different faiths to teach the whole range of subjects listed under the heading of "social sciences" without becoming entangled in theological debate. It can be done because it is being done almost without friction throughout the country. There surely is little difficulty in the elementary and secondary schools. Even in colleges and universities where the detailed study of historical and philosophic problems brings one face to face with warring theologies of the past and present, the situation can be handled, as current practice proves. All through our public school system from kindergarten to university we find that a complete secularization of education has operated with marked success. At the high levels the diversity of our religious convictions is reflected in the diverse faiths of our philosophers, historians, and social scientists. Those who wish to pursue the metaphysical aspects of theological discussions can do so within a scholarly framework. Those who are communicants of one faith find their spiritual homes in their respective churches.

Under our system any families who feel that secular education is a contradiction in terms are free to send their children to schools and colleges of a denominational character. If they do so, we who feel otherwise have only one reasonable request to make: Do not criticize the public schools or the nondenominational private schools ostensibly for this or that reason if you are really criticizing them for being secular. A frank discussion of the advantages and disadvantages of a secular versus a denominational school or college is to be welcomed. But continuous sniping at the former by "franc-tireurs" who do not publicly proclaim their real reasons for dissatisfaction ought to be condemned by all fair-minded persons.

We are now ready to consider the practical matters of school and college curricula in terms of history, philosophy, and the "social studies" (under this heading one usually groups ethics, political science, economics, psychology, sociology, and anthropology). At this point one may be quite pragmatic within wide limits whatever his or her religious beliefs; for one is concerned by definition with secular education. The theological component is to be supplied by the home and church. We can therefore talk in terms of behavior without being accused of embracing behaviorism as a philosophy. Those who subscribe to the significance of the question "What is man that Thou art mindful of him?" can nevertheless concede that the test of the secular education of a child is the subsequent behavior of the adult. As free citizens of a republic, irrespective of our religious beliefs, we are surely concerned not with what a man has studied but with what he does.

What is our ideal of the behavior of *all* American citizens irrespective of their trade? We may imagine a society in which each citizen, be he a skilled worker, a manager, a storekeeper, a professor, or a farmer, would have the minimum interest in his own or other people's occupational status, the maximum interest in how far his own or other people's conduct approximated the universally recognized ethical ideal. This ideal might be epitomized by such phrases as individual integrity in dealing with other people, human sympathy and moral courage. We imagine further that, to a much greater extent than now, parents would be interested in the future of their children, not in terms of providing privileges or special opportunities or an increased standard of living, but in seeing that they developed as trustworthy human beings whose place in the economic and cultural life of the country is commensurate with their abilities and their tastes. All of which implies no diminution in the pioneer spirit of adventure and zest for work. On the contrary, the goal must be a nation in which the citizens are not idly enjoying the heritage of the past but are eager for that change which is the birthright of a free people seeking new insights and anxious to apply new knowledge. And last but not least, we imagine that to a far greater degree than now men and women in our future more perfect society will have more interest in translating the neighborly spirit, for which Americans are rightly famous, into wise collective action both as individuals and as a nation; there will be a new approach to international affairs, a diminution of parochial prejudices, less "gang politics," less despoiling of the public treasury, fewer completely selfish pressure groups, more self-sacrificing men in public office — in short, a much healthier body politic.

Now, if we have agreed to formulate our ideals along some such lines, our aim must be to educate our present pupils so that they will act as adults in a way to forward those ideals. How is this to be accomplished? To what extent can we regard the process of education as similar to the experiments of the psychologist with animals during which conditioned reflexes are set up which determine subsequent behavior? To what degree should we develop a set of ethical and philosophical concepts in each youth which, formulated as ideals, will determine his or her action? How far can we regard allegiance to such abstract ideas as truth, justice, honor, as playing an important part in human conduct? In other words, is the devotion to principles a primary motivation or is reference to general principles nine times out of ten a rationalization of behavior? I raise these questions not to answer them but to illustrate the deep-seated issues involved in any thorough-going analysis of this phase of the philosophy of education.

To a not inconsiderable extent the disagreements about those educational topics which deal with human conduct reduce in the last analysis to metaphysical discussions. Surprising agreement may be found as to practical matters of curriculum and pedagogic methods; only when the reasons given are examined do the antagonists draw their philosophic daggers. But, even so, there

are issues in the field of ethics which ought not to be
ignored or glossed over even for the sake of peace. For
they are central, I believe, to the ideological conflict in
this divided world. If the first few chapters of this book
have any significance, those who plan our American
education must enter the twilight zone that separates
philosophy from theology far enough to come to grips
with the question of the basis for our ethics.

The skeptical behaviorist and the liberal Protestant,
for example, can go hand in hand in stressing the
Christian virtues, the one privately justifying ethical
teachings in terms of the development of a "normal"
individual and a smooth working society, the other by a
symbolic interpretation of the Christian dogmas. In
most situations the ideal behavior of an American citizen will be identically assessed by these two men. But
it is not difficult to envisage cases where the divergence
in basic philosophies will lead to different judgments.

Let us imagine two or three individuals on a raft or a
desert island with death certain in their eyes within a
few days or weeks. Under these conditions, which by
definition are isolated and mortally terminal, can an individual's conduct be said to be right or wrong? Where
by hypothesis there are no social consequences of action, is there any standard of reference for what occurs?
Is betrayal of a friend or even murder under these
highly unusual circumstances to be regarded only as a
physiological reflex and described as merely pleasing
or offensive to one's taste? Is behavior under these con-

ditions to be judged as right or wrong or merely regarded as similar to that of an insane person or an
animal?

These questions probe deeply into a man's outlook
upon the world; they throw a revealing light on the
common denominator which unites many Americans of
otherwise highly divergent views. For I am convinced
that all but a very small number of honest and intelligent citizens of all ages will answer these questions almost instinctively in just one way. They will affirm
that the universe is somehow so constructed that a sane
individual's acts are subject to moral judgments under
all circumstances and under all conditions. The nature
of the "somehow" is the door by which one passes into
a vast edifice of philosophical and theological discussion
— a mansion in which there are many chambers.

The reasons given for a belief in the significance of
the actions of even an isolated individual would be
many; but whether Protestant, Catholic, or Jew, active
church member or nonconformist, almost every American believes that human life is sacred. This fact is the
answer to those Cassandras who would have us think
that there is no spiritual unity in the United States.
When face to face with the question, is the dignity of
man determined solely by the fact that man is a social
animal, we automatically would say no. Our practical
democratic creed turns out on analysis to be an affirma-
tion of the common basis of our many faiths.

Theological and philosophic warfare between contending churches and rival groups obscures too often the unity of our culture. Instead of seeking to find broad terms in which to express the moral basis of our society, controversialists all too frequently argue as if their phrases alone had meaning. We quarrel about words which have different overtones for descendants of immigrants of different centuries and from different lands. This is unfortunate to say the least. For these are days when we must meet an aggressive Soviet ideology on the one hand, and face the possibility of a recrudescence of fascism on the other. We endanger our political and social solidarity if we close our eyes to the nature of the spiritual unity of this nation. You can argue the case for our free society up to a point in terms of the advantages to man as a social animal. But once the old battle cry "the state is in danger" is raised, what is the answer to the revolutionist or reactionary who would suppress all minorities? Why is it important to safeguard the rights of people with whom the majority does not agree? Those who base their case on history, utilitarian ethics, and practical politics can be stanch defenders of the American tradition of civil liberties. But those who affirm that our passionate adherence to the doctrine of personal liberty is a consequence of our belief in the sacrosanct nature of the individual have a still stronger case. To argue that the rights of the individual are a purely utilitarian invention is to deprive the characteristic American ideal of its cutting edge. You can build a free nation on an Hebraic-Christian view of human nature. You can destroy it by substituting another.

The contrast between the two ethics which are involved in the conflict of ideologies has been summed up by Arthur Koestler in his well-known novel, *Darkness at Noon*. In a striking dialogue one of the characters states the fundamental choice of the twentieth century in these words:

> There are only two conceptions of human ethics, and they are at opposite poles. One of them is Christian and humane, declares the individual to be sacrosanct, and asserts that the rules of arithmetic are not to be applied to human units. The other starts from the basic principle that a collective aim justifies all means, and not only allows, but demands, that the individual should in every way be subordinated and sacrificed to the community. . . .

At another point in the dialogue the same speaker, a supporter of the totalitarian view, inveighs against what he calls the "humanitarian *fog-philosophy*" in these words:

> Consider a moment what this would lead to, if we were to take it literally; if we were to stick to the precept that the individual is sacrosanct, and that we must not treat human lives according to the rules of arithmetic. That would mean that a battalion commander may not sacrifice a patrolling party to save the regiment.

But his companion objects, "Your examples are all drawn from war — that is, from abnormal circumstances."

To which the totalitarian replies:

Since the invention of the steam engine the world has been permanently in an abnormal state; the wars and revolutions are just visible expressions of this state. . . .The principle that the end justifies the means is and remains the only rule of political ethics; anything else is just vague chatter and melts away between one's fingers. . . .

These few sentences give us in short compass the basic conflict between the followers of the Soviet philosophy on the one hand and the believers in the "Christian and humane" ethics on the other. To many of us the whole story of human history would be only a "tale told by an idiot" and life would be devoid of meaning if its prime significance lay in the visible results of an individual's or a nation's actions. Whether a man lives or dies in vain can never be measured by the collective activity of his fellows. It can be measured only by the way he faces his own problems, by the success or failure of the inner conflict within his soul. For centuries Christians have quarreled as to the answer to the question: "What is man that Thou art mindful of him?" and I am inclined to think they will continue to disagree on this subject for many generations more. But it is the assertion implied in this question, not the answer, that is basic to any faith. And it is this assertion that gives significance to the individual, that makes imperative the concept of human liberty and provides the moral basis of a society of free men.

The study of man in our American schools must therefore start with certain postulates. The first is the sacrosanct nature of the individual; the second, an individual's obligation to other individuals; the third is that our type of society requires a high degree of personal liberty and at the same time active and sympathetic coöperation toward certain ends. These postulates should be placed in their historic setting. They should be developed as given elements in our culture. Not until the late school years or the college level need the philosophical background be explored. In the meantime, the families and the various churches will have developed a parallel set of explanations as to why these postulates must be taken as fundamental to our culture. History rather than philosophy is the medium for the transmission of our culture to the growing child in so far as secular education is concerned.

If this be granted, there need be no further argument as to the central place of American history in the "common core" of studies. There will be much discussion, however, about the way in which the study of the past of this country is to be related to the history of other nations and to current affairs. I do not propose to enter into a treatment of this and other pedagogic problems. In all except the most old-fashioned schools which still cling to the classics as the central core, a considerable amount of time is devoted to a study of the economic, political, and social problems of the day. And to a lesser or greater degree such studies of the contemporary world are related to some knowledge of the past. For example, a recent set of specifications for the last three years of high school in *Education for All American Youth* calls for a fourth of the total school time for subjects which fall under the head of "Education for Civic Competence." One may estimate that half of this time in turn is devoted to what are essentially matters of history.

As one proceeds from high school to college, the whole approach to general education must take into account the increased maturity of the student. It must also take into account the diversity of occupational goals. This last point has already been dealt with at some length in the preceding chapter. As far as the study of man is involved, one may venture to say that the philosophic element should become more and more predominant. Under whatever titles the student is led to consider all those topics which are often grouped together as the social studies or social science, the emphasis must shift toward the type of analysis that probes deeper and deeper into the premises. More and more abstract ideas and uncommon concepts should be introduced into a discussion of material which the same student four years earlier will have considered in a descriptive manner. Formal study of such subjects as economics, political theory, psychology, sociology, logic, ethics, and metaphysics must be reserved for college work and probably restricted to only certain types of colleges.

One may well pause from time to time in any exposition of an outline for general education and recall certain fundamental presuppositions. We are considering, let us remember, in this and the preceding chapter, education apart from its relation to an occupation in so far as such a separation can be made. Within the limits imposed by the heterogeneity of our population, we are trying to develop a program for general education for *all* American youth. The study of literature and art was given high rank in such an endeavor because of the way these studies develop socially healthy individuals: they provide the enduring satisfactions which stabilize the emotional life of modern man. So, too, do philosophy and history. These subjects may play a twofold role in education; they both enrich a life of contemplation and prepare a citizen for action. It is no accident that professors are always quarreling as to whether history and philosophy are to be classed under the humanities or along with economics and political science under the social sciences.

A set of common beliefs is essential for the health and vigor of a free society. And it is through education that these beliefs are developed in the young and carried forward in later life. This is the social aspect of general education, one might say. The future citizens we desire to educate should have strong loyalties and high civic courage. These loyalties ought to be to the type of society we are envisaging and to the United States as the home of this society. Such emotional attitudes are in part the product of a common knowledge and a common set of values. One of the tasks of the public schools is to evoke these loyalties through the medium of formal study. Educators often tend to overemphasize, however, the significance of the rational argument and the knowledge transmitted through books.

The war has underlined the fact that the most effective loyalties are often to small groups of men bound together by a common experience and a unity of immediate purpose. A unifying faith is in such instances not a matter of words or intellectual concepts but of a direct relationship between men. What we mean by democracy may be illustrated for some people better by action than by words.

For this reason the present emphasis in many public schools on "democratic living" is of the first importance. I should place high in the priority list of goals to be achieved by every teacher the inculcation of what we Americans call a "democratic attitude," a lack of snobbery. A loyalty to the type of society we are slowly endeavoring to shape on this continent can be evoked to the extent that the school itself is a society exemplifying the ideals we extol. To that degree we tend to win the loyalty of even the most ruthless individuals in the group. And there is a good chance that this loyalty will be transferred later to the nation.

We assume that our system of education aims to provide a high degree of fluidity in the social structure. We hope it may do so by providing greater equality of educational opportunity and by minimizing the differentiation between vocations — decreasing the visibility of the social structure. The two aims are closely allied. The kind of society we should aim to achieve is one where, more often than not, a boy or girl decides upon a career requiring advanced education because of a real interest, not in order to climb into a better economic or social group. The more we stress the multiplicity of significant careers and the importance of success in all manner of undertakings, the more we contribute to the prosperity of our nation.

From the point of view here presented, one of the most important jobs of the schools is to instill into the students the concepts not only of political but of social democracy. And this must be done in every grade. Here again we must recognize that the school is only part of a total social situation; many factors other than the teachers and the curriculum will determine the attitudes of the students. But the weight of the school should be thrown heavily against all forms of snobbery. General education for American democracy, let us never forget, is to be tested in terms of adult behavior. We postulate as our goal a free self-governing republic with a social structure as mobile as possible, and becoming more fluid every year. The social behavior in and out of the classroom, the ethical and social implications of the formal studies will be of first importance; "democratic behavior" will be emphasized; the spirit of competition will be fostered, but the concomitant evils will be mitigated by repeated emphasis on the many significant activities in which an adult may play a part; the spirit of snobbery will be reduced by minimizing the importance of any one hierarchy of social values.

On this latter point the times are with us: many social and economic currents are working to break down social barriers. In terms of rate of pay, for example, it seems likely that many white-collar jobs are going to be even less attractive in the future than they were in the past. Throughout this country a great movement has been in progress which tends to minimize the cultural differentiation between vocational and income groups. An interesting illustration of this, which has had enormous influence on the advanced education of women, is the change in status of the unmarried daughter. Time was, within the memory of many of us, when the economic level of a family (or of one branch of a family as compared to another) could be almost automatically gauged by noting whether the Misses So-and-So were ladies of leisure or were employed. It was assumed at the beginning of this century that, if the family income permitted, the daughters, unless married, were to be concerned with the "finer things of life," the social amenities, travel and brilliant conversation if the proper social milieu could be arranged. For a poor relative who taught school, an understanding and sympathetic hand was to be offered with all the grace good breeding could command.

Today, with a few exceptions, all this is completely altered. The unmarried woman in her twenties who has no job of any sort (even if she gives the pay to a charity) is the one whom her contemporaries pity. In debating this issue nowadays one is not talking in terms of different social strata. The whole status of a woman *vis-à-vis* a job is no longer a matter of economics; it is no longer a sign of superior social standing to be a lady of leisure. As a consequence, there has been an enormous breaking down of social barriers among young women, a mixing up of different groups. One may note in passing that it seems doubtful whether we have as yet assimilated the consequences of this social revolution into our thinking about the advanced education of young women. But that is a special aspect of education with which I do not propose to deal.

Many other illustrations could be given of the almost revolutionary social changes which have been taking place in this country in the last fifty years. Nearly without exception they have tended toward spreading the material and cultural dividends of our civilization among a wide variety of occupations. In terms of current pay, eventual security, conditions of work, and social standing this century has seen the disappearance of the relative advantages of government officials, judges, teachers, scholars, curators, librarians, and even members of the clergy. The position of craftsmen, skilled laborers of all sorts, workers in factories, and even many kinds of clerical employees has correspondingly improved. There seems every indication that this is not a temporary situation. On the contrary, the effects of this recent social revolution have hardly yet been appreciated; it will be a generation or so before we adjust some of our basic ideas to the new conditions.

On the whole our educational planning has kept pace with the changes; but by no means all of our educational thinking. Indeed, it is this discrepancy between fact and theory which now bedevils so much of the discussion of education. Distinguished scholars from Britain, for example, still write delightfully for American audiences about schools and colleges. But the premises of their arguments have almost no relation to the realities of the United States in the 1940's. If one accepts the view that education is a social process, general education must be responsive to changing times. The issue to which the bewildered layman might well direct his attention is the fundamental relation of formal instruction to the social pattern of the community. If he likes to deal in absolutes, he will refuse this offer and insist, instead, on examining the various current remedies offered for our educational ills. If, on the contrary, he has an inquiring mind he will consider the evidence presented both by history and the current scene, and judge accordingly.

This chapter and the preceding one on general education are in essence a plea to the citizen to reëxamine his own presuppositions and probe our educational problems with diligence and care. If he does this, one may or may not agree with his conclusions, but there is no real basis for a quarrel. Doctrinaires can never find a basis for accommodation; but men whose opinions are based on examination of evidence, while often in conflict, are always in communication. This attitude seems essential for the successful planning of public education by the citizens of this country in these troubled years.

7

GENERAL EDUCATION:
THE NATURAL SCIENCES

Unlike the two preceding chapters on general education, this chapter can be brief. Far less controversy is
involved in placing science in a school or college program than in the case of the humanities or the study of
man. Not that there are no formidable pedagogic problems. Quite the contrary. As I hope to show, we are a
long way indeed from finding a satisfactory answer to the
question: How can a nonscientist achieve an understanding of science? But there are no deep-seated issues
in this field comparable to those examined in the last two
chapters. This is an ancient battleground once fought
over with vigor but now only a reminder that even
academic wars sometimes end. I know of no one today
who challenges the thesis that some instruction in the
physical and biological sciences must be included in
school and college. The reasons given will represent a
variety of opinions, but the importance of teaching
science is granted by almost everyone.

Such being the case, one need not detain the general
reader long by a discussion of the problems in this area,
however difficult they may appear to those of us who
are immersed in the task of trying to find solutions. A

few paragraphs may be in order, however, to differenti-
ate clearly between science as part of a general education
and science as part of a professional education. Especially in the last year of high school and the first years of
college there is considerable confusion on this point. I
shall have something to say in the next chapter about
the study of science and particularly mathematics as a
basis for professional work. There I shall stress once
again the importance of finding the specially gifted youth
and giving him adequate high school preparation. But
here I am concerned only with general education, the
education for *all* American youth. What part should the
study of physics, chemistry, geology, astronomy, biology, play in this undertaking?

Various arguments have been advanced from time
to time by those who feel that the study of science has
been neglected by our schools and colleges. The oldest
of these is typical of the nineteenth century; it assumes
that an acquaintance with these subjects "trains the
mind" in some special way of great importance for modern man. The proponents of this view today are much
less vocal than half a century ago, but they are still to
be found in both scientific and educational circles. A
few, indeed, believe passionately that all rational and
relatively unprejudiced inquiries are scientific. They
maintain that there is a continuous transition between
those problems which yield to the labors of the scientific
investigator or the engineer, and all the vexing questions
which confront men and women in factories, offices, and

political gatherings as well as in the nursery, the kitchen, and the garage. A distinguished American scientist, for example, has recently written: "Men and women effectively trained in science and in the scientific method usually ask for the evidence, almost automatically. They have some of the experience and more of the critical judgment necessary to evaluate the evidence." One cannot help wondering where the author of this categorical statement obtained his evidence. I should have supposed that only a very exhaustive study of reactions and attitudes of many people with and without scientific training of various sorts could possibly supply the data from which such a generalization could arise. No such study has been made. In its absence, the skeptic will prefer the conservative assumption that there is little or no "transfer of training" from the scientific to the nonscientific activities of man. And he will buttress his position with an appeal to his own experience that as human beings scientific investigators are distributed over the whole range of human folly and wisdom in much the same proportion as other men.

Indeed, the skeptical educator may go even further and apply his corrosive acid to the phrase "scientific method." He will challenge the two assumptions that one finds in many arguments on education, namely, that an exact and impartial analysis of facts is possible only in the realm of science, and that exposure to science will produce a frame of mind that makes for impartial analysis in all matters. He will recall the history of the natural sciences (the physical and biological sciences), and with a certain relish refer his enthusiastic scientific friends to the violent polemics with which this history teems. To him it will appear that only very gradually did science become a discipline in which impartial and unprejudiced inquiry was assumed as a matter of course. Only after the scientific societies of the seventeenth century had been in operation for several generations did the cultural pattern of science assume its modern form. Not till then did the polemics of "philosophical inquiry" so reminiscent of theological debate yield to precise and unemotional scientific reports. The scientist today, of course, places little reliance on persuading his opponent with rhetoric or on driving him from the field with invectives. For his jury is a large body of well-informed peers and to them he need merely present exact facts as impartially as he can.

The reader may well accuse me of making too much of an academic point. For, as will be evident shortly, I am not opposing the inclusion of a considerable amount of natural science in the program of general education. Why bother about a disagreement as to the reasons for studying science, he or she may say, if everyone is agreed as to the answer to the practical question. But it is not so simple as this. For to some extent the way the sciences are presented hangs on the acceptance or rejection of the argument for their inclusion. At the risk of being redundant, I shall pursue my analysis of the so-called scientific method still further. There is no doubt about it, this phrase is still in favor; almost every program of general education includes it.

Indeed, in the last twenty-five years, indoctrination in the scientific method has been put forward with more and more insistence as one of the primary aims of modern education. I am the last to decry the importance of science or to suggest that we should not attempt to make it as understandable as possible to the average citizen, but the slogan in question, I must confess, worries me. I frankly do not know what my friends and colleagues have in mind. For the explanation is usually appended that by the scientific method is meant something far more general than the methods by which the natural sciences have advanced: it is proclaimed as a way of looking at life; at times it seems almost a panacea for social problems. Now to put the scientist on a pedestal because he is an impartial inquirer seems to me quite erroneous. Such a procedure fails to recognize the important fact that the modern scientist inherits traditions that make impartiality on matters of *his* science almost automatic. Let him deviate from the rigorous role of impartial experimenter or observer at the risk of his professional reputation; he knows very well what has been the fate of other scientists who have allowed their emotional attachment to their own ideas to get the better of their judgment. He is surrounded by a cloud of witnesses, so to speak, who are part of his social setting. Under these circumstances even an unstable personality may within the rigorous confines of a laboratory science become an impartial and judicial inquirer. But once he walks out of the door of the research institute — then he is as other men.

As a matter of honest pedagogy, it seems to me that one of the first objectives in teaching the natural sciences is to show the frame of reference in which they now operate. By this I do *not* mean a pseudo-philosophic discussion of relativity or the quantum mechanics as allegedly related to free will. Not at all. These are extremely difficult matters best avoided except by the most skilled college teachers. Rather, I refer to what I have just outlined about the conditions of scientific inquiry, that is to say, the nature of the assumptions about the external world which are essentially those of common sense ("animal faith," to use the phrase of Santayana). In addition, one must consider the reproducibility of phenomena and the nature of prediction and, above all, the restricted type of phenomena with which controlled experiments are concerned. Then if we seek to spread more widely the desire to examine facts without prejudice and to glorify the bold and impartial inquirers of the twentieth century we should go to other fields than those of the natural sciences.

We should hold before our students as models those few who in the world of human affairs have courageously, honestly, and intelligently based their conclusions on reason and inquiry. Furthermore, rather than leave in the minds of the pupils the very dubious proposition that the methods of science are applicable to all

manner of practical human affairs, we should show how
legal methods of inquiry have been used in Anglo-Saxon
countries. Likewise, we must study the rational methods of merchants, manufacturers, soldiers, and statesmen which were employed with considerable success for
generations, long before any idolatry of the word "science" came over the academic horizon. Too many educators appear to underrate the amount of hard-headed
thinking which has been done by practical men in the
history of the human race. We must stress the significance of rational inquiry throughout our general education, but the identification of this type of inquiry with
science confuses rather than clarifies the presentation.

In the previous chapter I have spoken of the growing
importance of anthropology, sociology, and psychology
in the study of man. I am one of those who look forward
with confidence to rapid progress in these sciences. Even
today too little of their point of view and their findings
is presented as a part of general education. Nevertheless, I believe that no good educational purpose is served
by spreading the ambiguous title "social science" over
all the academic activities concerned with a study of
man. And positive harm is done by claiming that the
scientific method is going to save us. Indeed, something
close to fraud is being perpetrated when this method is
defined by implication as the process by which the
physical and biological sciences have reached their
present stage. I find quite inadequate the description
of the scientific method given by most social scientists.

To me it is not an accurate epitome of the way physics, chemistry, and biology have developed; I doubt the wide validity of this alleged method. Of course, as in certain other cases already examined, the quarrel may be largely one of words. But, if so, it is one involving the precise use of words. A sociologist, for example, has recently answered the question "Can science save us?" in the affirmative; it is not the physical sciences, to be sure, but the social sciences he has in mind. We can be "saved," however, only if we inculcate into our population "a rudimentary understanding of what is the nature of scientific method as applied to human affairs and a conviction that this is the only effective method of approach." With much of his treatment of social science I am inclined to agree, but to say he overstates his case would be a grave understatement. As an example of science as applied to human problems he discusses the Census Bureau. The relation of this type of admirable and important work to the methods by which the natural sciences have developed seems to me extremely remote. To use the blanket word "science" to cover diverse human activities only adds to the bewilderment of the public. I should like to restrict the use of the word "science" so that the overtones are the same in the academic world as on the street. In short, the procedures by which the physical and biological sciences have developed should be the criteria for the use of the word.

To my mind we would do well to recognize the omnibus nature of the category "social science." History, political science, and economics for the most part are so distantly related to either physics or biology as to warrant a separate classification. The phrase "cumulative knowledge" seems to me useful in this connection. Some years ago I ventured to propose a trisection of the secular world. Draping the mantle of Francis Bacon around me, I suggested we might do well in this century to distinguish between (a) cumulative knowledge, (b) philosophy, and (c) poetry. The operational test to distinguish the first area from the other two is relatively simple and quite obvious. Whenever it can be said with some assurance that earlier writers or practitioners, if brought to life today, would recognize the superior position of their successors, then we can speak of cumulative knowledge. By such a test one distinguishes between Plato on the one hand and Archimedes on the other, or between Milton and Harvey, or between Immanuel Kant and Newton.

Large portions of history and philology as well as all of archaeology fall under this definition of cumulative knowledge, as do the physical and biological sciences and mathematics (including symbolic logic). Our increasing knowledge of man as an individual and as a social animal, and all of the practical arts from mining through agriculture to government, are likewise included, provided, of course, there has been real progress.

The German word "Wissenschaft" is often used to cover this whole vast field. We can translate it by "science" if we choose. I think, however, that this broad use of the word is confusing. The word "science" has very definite connotations to laymen. These are today connected with only one branch of cumulative knowledge. I define science historically by equating it with the extraordinary activity which arose in Italy in the sixteenth century and spread to the rest of Europe in the seventeenth, and which in our time has flourished and proliferated with so much vigor. Around 1600 there was a change in point of view among learned men which was so marked as to be revolutionary. It was so regarded by the leaders of thought of the seventeenth century, who often spoke of the "new philosophy," meaning by that, experimental and observational science.

I place science within the area of cumulative knowledge, instead of regarding it as coextensive with it. According to my view, only in very recent times did science emerge from the other human activities which had been accumulating knowledge for thousands of years (though I recognize, of course, that one traces a sort of prenatal history of science back to the Greeks and even further). The characteristic of the new philosophy of the seventeenth century was that it sought to deal with those ideas or concepts which arose from controlled experiment or observation and in turn led to further experiment and observation. Science, thus defined, is to be regarded as a series of interconnected conceptual schemes which arose originally from experimentation or careful observation.

The test of a new concept is not only the economy and simplicity with which it can accommodate the then-known observations, but its fruitfulness. Science has a dynamic quality when viewed not as a practical undertaking but as a process of developing conceptual schemes. Science advances not by the accumulation of new facts (a process which may even conceivably retard scientific progress) but by the continuous development of new and fruitful concepts.

The definition of science I have chosen, I should like to emphasize, is entirely independent of the field of inquiry or of any application of the knowledge obtained. Parallel with the development of science in the last three centuries and a half there has been a rapid development of the practical arts. At first the two activities were largely independent in spite of the hopes of Francis Bacon and the new philosophers. Improvements in the art of working metals, of growing food, of making glass and ceramic materials, and even in increasing the destructive power of weapons, were little affected by the early scientific work. It is not until we get into the nineteenth century that we begin to see anything like the practical influence of scientific progress to which the first scientists so confidently looked forward. And it is only in the twentieth century that we have seen so close an interaction between advance in science and progress in the practical arts as to result in some popular misunderstanding about the relation of the two.

If there be any merit in my scheme of classification

and my definition of science, its usefulness lies in the analysis of educational problems. Academic subjects fall within the three categories I mentioned earlier. The study of the humanities for the most part falls within the category of poetry, except as historical and philological material is used, when we enter the field of cumulative knowledge. In the study of man we are clearly concerned with the other two categories — namely, cumulative knowledge and philosophy. I shall not attempt to draw the line within a hazy zone. But some of the scholars who are often classed as social scientists would seem to me to be rather social philosophers, while others like the historians are concerned primarily with the nonscientific aspects of cumulative knowledge.

Experience has taught me the importance at this point of emphasizing vigorously that I am not placing any halo over the words "progress" or "science." I trust the preceding chapters have made it evident that in terms of general education, poetry and philosophy are of vastly more importance than science or even the whole field of cumulative knowledge. One may make this statement even after admitting the profound alterations in our cosmology brought about by advances in astronomy, physics, and our reading of the record of the rocks. The alteration wrought by science since 1600 is hardly greater, however, than the one produced by the revolutionary discoveries of the archaeologist in the last hundred years. But the extension of our knowledge of the antiquity of man and our rewriting of ancient history need not impel us to place any branch of cumulative knowledge in a preferred position. Academic snobbery, on whatever grounds it may base its case, has no place in a discussion of general education.

To return now to the teaching of the natural sciences in school and college, we might profitably direct our attention not to the question of why we teach them, but how we should teach them. If we reject the extravagant claims for the scientific method as a modern Aladdin's lamp and question the validity of the assumption that the study of physics trains the mind of the future statesman, we are led to a study of science from a less pretentious angle. Looking towards our schools with their heterogeneous population, we recognize again the fundamental importance for educators of the driving power of curiosity. Whatever the student's background, to some degree he or she is curious about the world in which we live. And this world is full of the products of applied science. Furthermore, many of the natural phenomena can be "explained" in terms of the various natural sciences. For young pupils the presentation of general science in terms of understanding the earth, the atmosphere, the process of life, and to some degree modern technology, is the most likely way to arouse their interest. Such an approach is now commonplace in our public schools. Courses in general science in one form or another are introduced even as early as five or six years before graduation from high school. Obviously there are grave difficulties in this method. Criticism is consequently rife. A few of the points at issue may be of sufficient interest to warrant inclusion in this book.

The first brings us back to conflict between general education for *all* American youth and the special education of a gifted few for professional careers. As in the other school subjects, the professors in the colleges are "highly dissatisfied" with what the schools are doing. Nine times out of ten general education is really not at issue for the criticism turns on the adequacy or inadequacy of high school science and mathematics as a basis for further work in these subjects in college.

The second type of criticism is directed to the ways and means of accomplishing the desired objective, namely, giving some understanding of science to all future citizens of this republic. There are still many scientists and teachers of other subjects, too, who feel that exposure to a more or less orthodox course in physics, chemistry, or biology in the last two years of school is essential. The general courses are easily ridiculed as "scrambled science," "cafeteria science," and as being so superficial as to leave only a complete misunderstanding of what science is. While admitting the validity of much of this criticism, I feel that it too often reflects a failure to consider the realities of the high school problem. For the school with a high proportion of students headed for college, social pressures are probably adequate to make the conventional disciplines of physics, chemistry and biology good vehicles for general education. But remembering the fundamental fact that to teach any subject well the teacher must arouse a real interest, I doubt whether the general science approach can be avoided. That the textbooks and the teaching techniques can be enormously improved hardly anyone will deny. To this end, active coöperation is now going on between teachers of science in our colleges and our schools. The fruits of their labors should be manifest in another decade.

One of the difficulties in presenting science as part of general education at both the school and college level is that of selection. The progress in all the sciences in the last three hundred years has been so great that the factual information is enormous. Even the selection of the major principles to be expounded is no easy matter. And some of these principles are today so complicated and the reasoning so sophisticated that any elementary exposition is open to the charge not only of dogmatism but of distortion. When I used the word "explanation" a few paragraphs ago, I opened the door for a controversy. Most of us today would want to put quotation marks around this word and present science from a less dogmatic point of view than our predecessors of the late nineteenth century. Questions of the reality of atoms, molecules, electrons, neutrons, not to mention photons and light waves and three-dimensional space, we should want to postpone to a college course. And even at the college level some of us would doubt the student's ability to handle them adequately as part of science. Rather, we should direct our students to study philosophy to see the various types of current answers. Unlike the teachers of science of fifty years ago, most thoughtful scientists would agree with Morris Cohen's appraisal of the famous case of the Church against Galileo. The one mistake the Church made was to abandon its original position that the Copernican astronomy is a mere hypothesis for "it would now be seen in the light of the theory of relativity to be on irrefutable ground."

It is too much to expect high school teachers to handle the philosophic background of scientific problems. For the immature student, however, as in the case of the study of man, history may be a useful substitute for philosophy. Enough of the history of science might be introduced into any course so that the edge of the apparent dogmatism of the textbook or the teacher might be blunted. At least a warning should be conveyed to the pupils that there are difficult problems behind such simple ideas as time and space, and that while a conceptual scheme of relative simplicity makes classical optics an exact science, the "explanation" of light is an extremely complicated affair. Needless to say, these comments are not confined to the teaching of general science but are equally applicable to the conventional science subjects at the high school stage.

Since the present book is primarily concerned with our schools and not our colleges, I will spare the reader my own somewhat heterodox views as to the way science should be taught in college as part of a general education. I am convinced that the usual freshman course in physics, chemistry, biology, or even astronomy or geology is ill designed for this purpose. Such courses must be aimed at those who are majoring in science. For the others I am inclined to believe case histories drawn from the various sciences illustrative of different procedures should form the central core. Concentration on a few relatively simple illustrations with ample attention to the experimental and observational difficulties may convey to the future nonscientist some understanding of science, though perhaps it is an understanding of scientists that should be the prime objective of such a course. At all events, I refer any who may be interested in this subject to my Terry Lectures published by the Yale University Press and entitled *On Understanding Science: An Historical Approach.*

8

EDUCATION FOR A CAREER

Up to this point I have been concerned primarily with general education. While no sharp line divides general from vocational education, a separate consideration of the problems involved in formal training for a career is a necessary part of an analysis of the function of our schools. Let us start with the elementary grades.

Teaching the basic skills may be regarded either as part of general education or as training for an occupation. Inability to read and write and handle figures disbars one from all but the simplest forms of employment; it also makes impossible an individual's functioning as a citizen of this nation. One need not devote a line to arguing the importance of our schools as a means of insuring that all American citizens will be able "to read and write and do arithmetic." All the different varieties of educational philosophies agree on the importance of literacy and some degree of competence in handling arithmetic and algebra. How this literacy is to be accomplished and how much time should be devoted to this end in the schools is, of course, another matter. Here we encounter different educational theories and highly technical discussions on pedagogic matters.

Perhaps the greatest single cause of complaint con-

cerning our schools and colleges is on the score of the
inability of the graduates to express themselves adequately, either in speech or in writing. A second is our
dismal failure to awaken in more than a small fraction
of even our college students a continuing interest in
good literature and scholarly works dealing with history, philosophy, and science. To be sure, the best sell-
ers include non-fiction titles, and serious philosophic
and historical tomes sometimes are distributed in surprising numbers. But when one thinks of the total number of people in the nation over the age of sixteen who
can read, the most spectacular sales are seen to represent something very different from what is implied
by the statement, "Everybody has read that book." If
we compare the situation with England in the late
seventeenth and early eighteenth centuries, for example, it seems clear that the sale of Clarendon's *History of the Rebellion*, and *Burnet's History of His Own
Time* reached a far greater proportion of the total number of potential readers than any volume in this country
today. Newspapers and magazines are, of course, an
entirely different matter, and the circulation of some of
these serves to remind us of the number of citizens who
can read and do read, but who do not read many books.

This failure of our education at what is admittedly a
crucial point must be regarded, I believe, as only a passing phase. The phenomenon, however distressing, is another illustration of our difficulty in solving the problem
inherent in the educational dilemma already referred

to in previous chapters. By a series of approximations we have to discover how our schools in handling *all* American youth can nevertheless evoke as high a degree of literacy as is latent in each pupil. We are committed to a democratic undifferentiated education as far as possible. We seek for a "common core" of general education or a course of "common learnings" which will unite in one cultural pattern the future carpenter, factory worker, bishop, lawyer, doctor, sales manager, professor, and garage mechanic. The specifications for such a course have been laid down by one set of educators in *Education for* All *American Youth* as follows:

Common Learnings: A continuous course for all [during the last three years of high school and two years of college] planned to help students grow in competence as citizens of the community and the nation; in understanding of economic processes and of their roles as producers and consumers; in cooperative living in family, school, and community; in appreciation of literature and the arts; and in the use of the English language. Guidance of individual students is a chief responsibility of "Common Learnings" teachers.

We shall return to the question of guidance later. I quote this outline here to show that training in the use of the English language is included. But it is likewise included in the discussion of preparation for occupations. And when one is focusing attention on high school and post-high school education, perhaps it would be well to emphasize the importance of reading and writing in relation to future occupational goals. Certainly, the study of mathematics beyond elementary algebra and foreign languages must be so regarded. We are here again face to face with the fact that general education cannot be divorced from preparation for an occupation. The study of the humanities, we have already seen, must seek a new base if it is to fulfill its function in our unstratified society of the future. And the development of skills in writing and speaking goes hand in hand with a study of literature. Our success or failure therefore in answering the challenge in one area will affect the outcome of our efforts in the other.

Until such time, however, as a considerable change has taken place in the presentation of art and literature to *all* American youth, we would do well to stress the relation of the use of the English language to the subsequent career of the student. If this is done, to be sure, there must be a differentiation in the program in English in the high school years for students headed in different directions just as there must be options in mathematics, foreign languages, and science. One of the reasons for the failure of our schools to lay a proper foundation for the use of the English language may reside in the fact that we have been too anxious to use this study as one of the elements of the "common learnings." Writing cannot be separated from reading; and as yet the motivating forces are lacking to awaken real enthusiasm for literature in many young boys and girls.

Distaste for conventional studies coupled with lack of aptitude seems to be pretty widely and uniformly distributed throughout the economic scale. But in the upper income groups, we must remember, strong social forces are brought to bear to make "little Johnnie" get his lessons. And, in addition, the schools to which Johnnie goes will not only supplement the parental pressure to do better in his studies, but will provide a great deal of pleasant extracurricular education as well. As a result, the total experience is an exposure, at least, to a wide range of literature; those who have been thus exposed for the most part have had an interesting and pleasurable social experience with their fellows. Both in speaking and in writing they tend to conform to a pattern which provides them with a certain degree of mastery of the English language. Granted that the results even here leave much to be desired, the question seems to be how similar motivation can be found under other social and economic conditions.

At this point we touch once again upon a topic which has been more than once mentioned in passing: selection of gifted youth at a relatively early age in education. The educational dilemma, of course, looms above the horizon; differentiation versus undifferentiated curricula is on the agenda for discussion. The private preparatory schools and some of the suburban high schools, by and large, plan their programs on the assumption that 85 or more per cent of their students will go on to a four-year college, university, or institute of technology. Therefore, consciously or unconsciously, their general education and specialized education are focused on a single objective. They are intended as a first step down a road which leads to the learned professions and the managerial positions in business. There is far from being agreement, of course, as to what should be the content of such college preparatory courses, but the variations in opinion all fall within certain tacit premises which we inherit from a previous era. Teachers and professors may quarrel about whether ancient or modern foreign languages should occupy a prominent position; whether physics, chemistry, and biology should be school or college subjects; and how far mathematics should be required of all. But these are details relatively easy to settle in a school that is homogeneous as regards occupational goals. The difficult question is how a brilliant boy or girl, clearly professional material, should be educated in a high school where not more than 30 per cent of the graduates wish to go on for further education.

Nine out of ten of the critics of our public high schools never understand the significance of this issue. They talk as though one could insert a curriculum designed for one type of school, the preparatory school, into another social setting. Those with experience have long ago given up the attempt; they have not abandoned differentiated curricula in the high schools, but have tried not only to develop common learnings which cut across all the programs, but also to find motivations for the college programs which correspond to the realities of the school in question. In this very difficult process the best interests of the talented youth may have been neglected (I am inclined to think they have), but that secondary education has been "ruined," as some declare, is certainly not the case. Those who bemoan the fact that most high school programs are not identical with those of the preparatory high schools are simply refusing to admit that education is a social process. They try to transfer what may be sound educational practice in one situation to another only distantly related.

Mathematics, foreign languages, and sciences I have already indicated are to be regarded as subjects to be studied primarily with a view to the subsequent career of the individual. A student of marked ability in a school from which the graduates go to college as a matter of course may well devote much time to a thorough training in languages and mathematics. For the future member of the learned professions such a preparation will be of value. His college years can be free of elementary work in these skills and thus time be found for the more philosophic approaches to history, literature, and science (including the sciences of man). On the other hand, if this is not possible within the framework of the school, either the student must go without or spend a considerable portion of his college course on subjects which could have been studied earlier.

Fortunately, for a really able student the time necessary to acquire a reading knowledge of a language in college by no means coincides with that usually allotted to the study of the language in school. His capacity coupled with a greater degree of maturity and the increased tempo of college work means that not as many hours are sacrificed as would at first sight seem to be required. This fact repeatedly demonstrated has led one group of public school men to advocate the elimination of all foreign languages (modern and ancient) from the high schools. To me this is going much too far. In a world in which this country must be ever more conscious of other nations, linguistic skills are as important as mathematical ability and scientific and artistic talent. The boys and girls who can learn a new language rapidly should be found young, and developed. Granted this is possible only in those schools where advanced education is in the air, the matter is none the less important.

Here is a good example of what guidance can do if properly employed. There is considerable evidence to indicate that linguistic and mathematical ability can be recognized in the early high school years; musical talent, of course, makes itself apparent much earlier. We have long been accustomed to discovering the unusual boy or girl in the artistic field and we are providing more and more for the education of such talent within the school. But relatively little is done along parallel lines for those who have comparable talent in languages and mathematics. Yet how much society has to gain by the early recognition of such people and their adequate education!

The development of better tests for sorting out students according to various aptitudes is now a matter of great concern. As these tests improve and the whole work of guidance expands, we can hope that the specially gifted youth will be recognized to an ever-increasing degree and his or her education will be given more attention. Guidance is of prime importance in the transition from school to college, but it has an equally important function in the high schools. All laymen who wish to improve our public schools should be vitally interested in the support of this phase of education and the scientific investigations which are at its base.

One may hazard the opinion that the content of the secondary school curriculum is not as important for the talented youth as either the defenders of the classical tradition or the innovators of modern times would sometimes have us think. Leaving aside the special preparation in mathematics and in physics now generally required for admission to institutes of technology or undergraduate engineering schools, the minimum skills which should be developed by the time a boy or girl of more than average intellectual ability has reached the age of 17 should be: writing English, handling mathematics in so far as arithmetic and algebra of an elementary sort are concerned, and ability to read with concentration and some degree of understanding. All three of these are by no means easy to achieve, and in many schools probably more time should be devoted to these minimum essentials. The fact remains that the record of boys in liberal arts colleges where a variety of programs of study are available fails to demonstrate the superiority of one type of school curriculum over another in so far as college work is concerned. Irrespective of former schooling, brilliant students show a remarkable ability to do outstanding work. Of course, if a student has never studied a foreign language before entering college and if a knowledge of a foreign language is desired, college time must be used for that purpose. A similar situation exists in regard to advanced mathematics. But that is another story.

The three criteria which I would suggest as the measure of the effectiveness of a secondary school from the point of view of a *gifted boy* would be as follows. First, the intellectual interests of the student must be keenly stimulated during the entire last four years of his school work. This is of the first importance. If it can be done in a given school by studying the classics, that is an argument in favor of that school; if it can be achieved in another by studying American history as related to the current scene, or in a third by early and intense exposure to science as tied into the modern mechanized world, no one should quarrel too severely with these programs. The boys thus stimulated are likely to enter college with a zest for intellectual adventure; and this zest, it must be admitted, is all too rarely found.

The second criterion would be the inculcation of a belief in the relevance of formal study and "book learning" to the problems of the day. One of the chief aims of the modern method of handling the so-called social studies is some such goal. The attempt to relate the study of history, ethics, elementary political theory, to the current problems of the time is well founded, to my mind, because of the importance of developing such an attitude. Continued emphasis on the importance of rational analysis and the value to be obtained by reference to our accumulated knowledge is the basis of the use of reason in the modern world. Some would call this training in the scientific method, but as I have already indicated I think such use of the phrase ill advised. I would rather speak of rational inquiry. The old-fashioned schools are apt to be deficient in this respect; this is perhaps their weakest point. The objective is to implant in young minds a firm belief that there is a relation between scholarly work and the complex and baffling problems of the modern world. Convinced of this while young, a student going on to college will relate his work there to the problems of the day, and continue to do so in adult life as well. All too often in the past, students have regarded the modern world as something entirely apart from what was studied out of books. Classical education as usually presented in preparatory schools has suffered from this defect. Except for the handful of students who have a special aptitude for language and an unusual bent for literature it fails to arouse enthusiasm for intellectual adventure.

My third criterion for judging a school would be the work habits that are acquired by the student. The ability to knuckle down and do a hard intellectual job, the willingness to go through drill in order to appreciate or understand something to which it leads, is essential for advanced education. On the whole, the old-fashioned schools can claim to do better on this point than those with modern curricula. But all through school and college I think the old pedagogic principle is thoroughly sound that no effective teaching can be achieved without first interesting the students in the subject taught. Relatively small classes and stimulating teachers are the prime requisites of all teaching, whatever the type of high school. This is much more important than the problem of the content of the curriculum or even the pedagogic methods that are employed. In terms of the public schools large expenditures of the taxpayers' money are required. There can be no escape from this conclusion, and the lay critic of the schools must constantly keep the cost of good teaching in his mind.

The necessity for good teaching is so obvious as to require no special emphasis in connection with either general education or education for a career. The problem of recruiting the members of the teaching staff and their adequate training is, however, full of difficulties. Perhaps the greatest single change that one could hope for in the immediate future would be a burying of the hatchet between the professors of liberal arts colleges and so-called professional educators. The two feuding parties have been on the one hand those who profess a knowledge of subjects, and on the other those who profess a knowledge of education, or are teaching in our public schools. Conditions may have improved somewhat in the last few years, but the need for a "truce among educators" still seems apparent. As a basis for this truce I once proposed a set of armistice conditions. I repeat them here for the benefit of any teachers or professors who may read this book (the layman is advised to skip them).

1. Let it be agreed by the professors in our colleges and universities that the high schools of the country today have a job to do which is not to be measured primarily in terms of their success or failure in the formal education of the specially gifted youth.

2. Let it be admitted that by and large a good job has been done in providing an education for a large proportion of American youth and that the present movement along such lines as those indicated in the volume, *Education for All American Youth*, is in the right direction.

3. Let the professors in the faculties of arts and sciences agree to find out more about the real problems facing the high schools of the country and the type of education which should be supplied to that vast number of boys and girls for whom a four-year college or university is far from being the proper educational channel.

4. Let the faculties of education and the superintendents of schools and those concerned with secondary education agree that in attempting to solve the tremendous problems of the last fifty years they have neglected a number of important matters which concern

the type of youth who should in the best interest of the nation go on to college.

5. Let those concerned primarily with high school education agree (a) to explore more sympathetically the ways and means of discovering special talent at an early age; (b) to provide a stronger motivation among many groups to evolve a greater degree of intellectual curiosity; and (c) to provide better formal instruction for those of high scholastic aptitude — all this to be accomplished without a segregation which might turn the boys and girls in question into either prigs or academic snobs.

6. Let the schools agree that if the colleges will give up many of their formal requirements for admission in terms of content of courses (as certain of the Eastern colleges have done already), they in turn will be willing to rate their students continuously in terms of scholastic aptitude. Thus, if the college can no longer count on adequate training in special skills, it may know better than ever before that it is choosing potential brains.

To the extent that the objectives of this truce may be accomplished, many difficult questions connected with the training of teachers may be answered. For anyone at all familiar with academic prejudices will realize how devastating in its effects has been the academic civil war which has been going on for several decades on almost every campus. To trace the origin of this war among educators would be to restate what has been said earlier about the growth of public education in the

United States. The reader must bear in mind not only the enormous expansion in numbers in our schools but the change in composition of the student body of the high schools. In the 1880's the high schools and their equivalents — the private academies and preparatory schools — were essentially institutions for preparing young people for entrance into college. No one who has read thus far in this volume needs to be reminded how radically different is the situation at the present time.

If we examine historically the expansion of public education and the change in the nature of the school population, we run into an interesting question: What institutions were to supply the teachers required to tackle the new and formidable pedagogic problems? Whose responsibility was it to think through the educational implications of the vast social change? One may say it should have been the job of the colleges and universities. But do we find that the faculties of arts and sciences were active in this matter? Do we find that they endeavored to train teachers and superintendents who would wrestle with these vast problems? Do we find professors of science, linguistics, and the social sciences sitting up nights thinking how best to answer these educational questions of so much moment to the country? With a few noteworthy exceptions, the answer is an emphatic no. All the evidence indicates that the faculties of arts and sciences in our colleges during this period of rapid change and expansion confined themselves to bemoaning the situation.

It was left to the schools of education or departments of education in the colleges, particularly to Teachers College in New York, to see how the demands could be met, to discover what were the best ways to educate teachers to handle the new burdens America had placed upon them.

Historically the liberal arts colleges abdicated, and teachers colleges and schools of education took over the job. They were the inheritors of the separatist tradition of the earlier normal schools. When university professors blame the schools of education for the shortcomings of our public schools, the reply from the professors of education in historical terms is all too evident. But while the origin of the quarrel is of significance, the important matter is not to assess blame but to work for close coöperation in the future. One way that this may be accomplished has already been suggested. In the past, the psychologists more than any other members of the usual college faculty have been interested in the problems of the schools; they have worked with and in schools of education. In the future we may hope that not only psychologists but sociologists and social anthropologists will follow this same coöperative path. In this direction lies the hope for progress not only in establishing peaceful relations between faculties but in improving the basis of our understanding of education as a social process. Barring the advent in the educational world of another great figure like John Dewey, who was both an academic philosopher and a leader of professors of education and school teachers, this building of a bridge between certain scientific disciplines and the schools of education seems the most likely way to improve the training of our teachers. The importance of this understanding will be evident to all who have followed my argument thus far.

We may now turn to a brief consideration of subject matter. Among the serious faults which professors find in our public schools is the teaching of mathematics. The professors who complain on this score are, of course, those who teach mathematics and science. They were delighted to find an ally in the military during the last war. The tests showed that there was much to be desired in the ability of the average high school graduate to handle numerical problems, let alone demonstrate any competence in algebra. Here again is evidence of the price we pay for the undifferentiated schooling during the early years of school.

All along the line the teaching in our high schools must be improved, almost everyone would agree to that. But in addition there must be more attention paid to the grouping of students according to ability, even in such subjects as mathematics. One could repeat much of what has already been written in connection with the study of English — the need for relating the study to the subsequent career of the student. If one felt that the only way to get a higher degree of mathematical competence among college freshmen was to hammer home to *all* high school students arithmetic, algebra, and geometry in the old-fashioned way, the case would be hopeless.

The teaching of English, foreign languages, and mathematics must be made more effective. To do so, however, requires not a return to the older methods but an imaginative approach to the radically new conditions which are present in our schools today. Keeping fast to the principle of the minimum of differentiation and with a realistic appraisal of the role of occupational uncertainties, teachers and administrators should seek to improve the preparation of those who should proceed to the professions. The nation needs men and women well educated in specific careers almost as much as it needs citizens with a proper general education for democracy.

In the preceding chapter the study of the natural sciences was considered as part of a general education. To round out the picture a few words are necessary at this point as to the study of the physical and biological sciences in high school as part of a preparation for a career. We are here concerned with that group of students destined for four-year colleges or universities. The occupations which require some specialized knowledge of one or more of the natural sciences are, in addition to careers in the sciences themselves, engineering, medicine, agriculture, nursing, and various technical semi-professions connected with science and its application. It is impossible to become a professional in any of these areas without having studied at least one orthodox course in physics and chemistry at the college level.

This being so, the question often arises, what should be the high school preparation for college work in science viewed as part of a professional education?

On this point as on so many others, the teachers and the professors find themselves quite frequently in disagreement. In part this disagreement stems from the dissatisfaction of the college men with the way science is taught in the high school and in part from a difference in the appraisal of the value of fundamental instruction in physics, chemistry and biology before a student has reached the freshman year of a four-year course. Most university instructors interested in students concentrating in science and engineering would probably prefer a solid foundation in mathematics to even the best school instruction in the physical sciences. Probably it is also safe to say that the majority of chemists and biologists would give preference to high school physics in choosing the ideal preparation for a freshman course. But even the best testing and guidance can hardly succeed in predicting the subsequent careers of high school students so accurately as to foretell who is to concentrate in science. Unless a boy or girl in high school has much difficulty with mathematics or has a strong distaste for science, it might be safest to assume that he or she is likely to desire to study the natural sciences in college. That being so, two of the following three courses well taught should be included in the high school program: physics, chemistry, biology. Mathematics, of course, is of the first importance, and probably more talent is lost to the sciences pure and applied (including medicine) by the inadequacies of our schools in this field than in any other. There will be those who disagree with this judgment, but as both a former professor of chemistry and one who has heard evidence from colleagues in the other sciences concerned with freshmen from all over the United States, I venture to be dogmatic on a point where only a scholarly inquiry could really give the proper answer.

This chapter would not be complete without at least a recognition of a large section which remains unwritten. This should concern vocational training at the high school level. The demand for such training testifies to its importance. To repeat once more the obvious, we could not, if we would, force down the throats of *all* American youth even a diluted college preparatory course. We could not, if we would, separate into different school buildings those who wish to enter the professions via the universities and all others. Except in certain cities, our high school pupils come together in one school which serves a community. Such differentiation as is required will be within one school and should be so arranged as to create as little social distinction as possible. In some schools it will be the various vocational programs which attract the largest numbers, and in a few these offerings will have the highest prestige. In others it will be the university preparatory work. In those communities which continue the high school two years beyond the usual termination (the 13th and 14th grades) in a local two-year college, the vocational programs will provide for this extension. In such schools the general program — the common learnings — will likewise be continued in these two advanced years. The degree to which general education and vocational training can be combined is a matter of discussion and experimentation at the present moment. Much will depend on whether in the near future we are to look to a vigorous expansion of college enrollments, and, if so, what types of colleges will be involved.

Our consideration of education for a career has taken us beyond the problems of the secondary school. Before we can proceed further we must consider in separate chapters the whole question of general and special education in the colleges and universities.

9

THE UNIVERSITY

The critical period in a young man's life as far as the relation of his education to his career is concerned lies between the ages of sixteen and twenty-one. If he drops out of high school, or finishes high school and does not go on to a university, many roads are barred; for example, only with the greatest difficulty can he become a doctor, lawyer, or engineer. On the other hand, if he graduates from a four-year liberal arts college, in many cases he will consider that his "higher education" was thrown away if he takes up an occupation largely recruited from non-college men. Assuming for the moment that all barriers of economics and geography and national origins were swept aside by a magic wand, how would a wise educator proceed to plan the education of thousands of young men in any one of the forty-eight different states? Is everyone to go to college? If so, what kind of college? If not, on what basis are some to be denied "the privileges of a higher education"?

To my mind the crux of the problem is to be found in such phrases as "the privileges of a higher education." If we could eliminate the word "higher" we could at least make a start toward thinking more clearly about the relation of our colleges to the structure of American society. For the adjective "higher" implies at once that those who do not go to a university or a four-year college are forever on a lower plane. And any discerning teacher in our secondary schools will testify that the social implications of "going to college" weigh quite as heavily with parents and children as does proven aptitude for college work. Furthermore, any placement officer of a college knows full well that it is a rare holder of a bachelor's degree who is eager to take up as his lifework a trade or vocation for which he might have been trained in a technical high school.

In the last fifty years in many sections of the country the colleges have been considered to no small degree as vocational ladders (though many a professor would shudder at the term) not because of the intellectual content of their curricula or the training of the mind, but because of the "friends one made." The tendency of management to hire only college men as junior executives is merely one manifestation of the undefined but very definite recognition on the part of ambitious people that "without a college education you cannot get ahead." The practice of the Armed Services during the war and the public statements of some high ranking officers have increased this feeling. The extent to which such ideas confuse our thinking about education beyond the high school can hardly be exaggerated.

Let us eliminate all the hierarchical overtones from the word "higher" and get squared away for a discussion of high school and college in terms of the ideal of equality of educational opportunity. Instead of raising the question, "Who should be educated?" let us rather consider the problem, "How long should be the education of the members of each vocation?" Of course, those who consciously or unconsciously reject the premise of working toward a more fluid social order should stick to the phrase "higher education" and underline the adjective. Anyone who wishes to solve our educational problems along hereditary class lines is well advised to support an educational pattern in which collegiate training is primarily for students who can pay for it — this training to be suitable both for those who enter the professions and for those who are to be managers of industry and commerce. Public education would then be largely concerned with providing another type of terminal schooling for future clerical workers, still another for manual workers, and so on through a close-knit stratified social system. The exceptionally brilliant boy, measured in academic terms, can be taken care of under such an arrangement by a relatively inexpensive system of scholarships, or at least he can in theory.

On the other hand, if we want to move toward a more flexible social structure, we must consider the final years of formal education not as a privilege of those who can afford to pay, or to be won by a few with high scholastic skill — but something open to all who deserve it and *need* it. And the emphasis on the word "need" is all-important, provided we define "need" in terms of subsequent vocation.

It seems evident at first sight that certain vocations require longer periods of formal training than do others.

As now conceived, public health tops the list; medicine and the academic careers requiring a Ph.D. in arts or letters are next; research in science is not far behind; then come law and engineering — to name only a few of the well-recognized professions. All of these have demanded, in the past, at least four years beyond high school, medicine usually eight. Not only do these vocations require a long period of formal education, but the nature of the general as well as the specialized work corresponds to the orientation of the able student measured in terms of college grades. The path to these occupations might well separate from the main educational road at the end of high school. In the first years of this century this path was the main road and indeed almost the only way to the learned professions. The universities supplied professional education; the four-year colleges either as separate institutions or within the universities fed the university professional schools.

But, as already indicated, during the last fifty years the four-year colleges have been the pathway not only to the professions but to white-collar jobs in business. The number and nature of the professions have expanded, to be sure, and the success of the agricultural colleges has blurred the distinction in certain states. By and large the opinion that higher education is to be equated with a bachelor's degree from a four-year institution has been gaining ground for a generation.

I hope to show in this and the following chapter that this pattern can and should be altered. The time has come, it seems to many educators, when we must distinguish more clearly between professional training (the characteristic educational function of a university) and a combination of general education and vocational training which may be accomplished in local two-year terminal colleges. In presenting this thesis, it would be logical to consider the two-year college first and then go on to analyze the functions of a university. But such a procedure would be unrealistic, for today the two-year local college is still in the process of development whereas the university has already assumed a very definite status. Before urging reforms, therefore, which alter to some degree the accepted pattern of education beyond the high school, we need to examine the present state of advanced education in the United States. In particular, we must understand the history of American universities and the way their growth has reflected some of the characteristics of our society.

A century and a half ago no one could have foreseen that the university tradition as imported to this continent in the seventeenth and eighteenth centuries was to undergo a significant mutation. No one then could have predicted that exposure to the social and political climate of the United States, to alternate blasts of Jeffersonian and Jacksonian democracy in particular, was to bring about an academic revolution and that the state universities were to play a leading role in the transformation; but such was in fact the case.

Only in the last fifty years has the reality of the

change in species become apparent to all observers, and only in the last twenty-five years has the true significance of the alteration been widely understood. Even today there are those who regard the change as a mere temporary and extremely regrettable aberration to be attacked by drastic surgery — pruned or cut back, as it were, to conform to the older European model of a perfect university.

But what is this university tradition which has undergone a revolution in American hands — a revolution equivalent to a biological mutation? Indeed, what is a university? How shall we define the *genus*? For nearly a thousand years there have been universities in the Western World; to understand the present institutions, we must therefore comprehend something of their history. For while there have been several clear and distinct changes in the pattern, the essence of the university tradition has through all these years remained constant. We can describe a university, it seems to me, as a community of scholars with a considerable degree of independence and self-government, concerned with professional education, the advancement of knowledge, and the general education of the leading citizens. To accomplish these three ends, it has been found desirable often — but not always — to incorporate into the community of scholars a community of students. Thus arose what has been termed the "collegiate way of living." Thus came about the emphasis on what we now call the "extracurricular" educational values.

As the university tradition came to America, it was based on four ultimate sources of strength: the cultivation of learning for its own sake, the educational stream that makes possible the professions, the general educational stream of the liberal arts, and, lastly, the never-failing river of student life carrying all the power that comes from the gregarious impulses of human beings. According to my view, universities have flourished when these four elements have been properly in balance; on the other hand, when one or more of these same elements has diminished or dried up, the academies of advanced instruction have failed signally in performing a relevant social function.

The cultivation of learning alone produces not a university but a research institute; sole concern with student life produces in these days either an academic country club or a football team maneuvering under a collegiate banner; professional education by itself results in nothing but a trade school; an institution concerned with general education, even in the best liberal arts tradition, divorced from research and training for the professions is admittedly not a university but a college. Therefore, to my mind, the future of the American university depends primarily on keeping a balance between these four traditional elements of strength. These four elements were the basis of the properly balanced plan in a time when universities were flourishing; they must continue to be in balance if the American university is to fulfill its functions in the times that are to come.

But what is there new, one may ask, about the American university, and how does the novelty (if any) affect the prospects for its future? The mutation, I believe, occurred in two of the four historic elements of which I speak: namely, professional education, and general education of the leading citizens. The first was a change in content, an enormous growth; the second, a change in type of student. Both represent a vast broadening of the educational goals; both present us with problems still unsolved. The changes have been to a large degree unconscious responses to social forces, and often the rationalization of the transformations has been in other terms than I shall use.

As public secondary education expanded in the last decades of the nineteenth century and in the first half of the twentieth, the colleges and universities likewise expanded. Not only were the applicants more numerous, they were much more heterogeneous as to backgrounds and ambitions. Furthermore, the political, social, and economic development of the United States vastly altered the way in which the public regarded education. As the years went by, it became more and more evident that in our complex industrialized society mere ability to read and write, added to native wit, was not enough. With the passing of the frontier, the pioneer spirit was turned away from new lands toward new industries. And to manage modern industry requires more than a high school education — at least for all but the very exceptional man.

With increasing industrialization went increasing urbanization, a higher standard of living, and a vast number of services available for city and town dwellers, more and more new mechanical and electrical devices distributed widely among the population — automobiles, electric refrigerators, and radios, to mention the most obvious examples. All this industrial expansion required more and more men and women with a larger and different educational experience than would have been necessary fifty years earlier to run a farm, a store, or even a bank.

The pressure on the universities, therefore, to educate men and women for specific vocations both increased and diversified. Beginning with the Morrill Act, the public had recognized the need for education in agriculture and the mechanical and industrial arts. Many a state in the Union made the significant step of combining the new agricultural and industrial arts colleges with an older state college of arts and letters. Perhaps one could say that from this union came the new American university. But, if so, the transformation rapidly spread elsewhere. Even before the great influx in numbers, the pattern had been set in publicly controlled and privately controlled universities alike; the mechanical and industrial arts (later to be known as engineering) and agriculture were recognized as being on a par, at least in theory, with divinity, medicine, and law.

As the twentieth century grew older, both the enrollments in our universities and the diversity of the training increased with each decade. The word "profession" in danger of being stretched beyond the elastic limit, was supplemented by the phrase "semi-profession." But soon the voice of the critic was heard in the land. Able and distinguished citizens became alarmed at this transformation of the idea of a university in American hands. When you once abandon the concept of a university as a home of learning, a place where the life of the mind is to be cultivated at all costs, you destroy our centers of higher education, they declared.

But in spite of those outcries and lamentations, the development proceeded on its way. One of our oldest universities strengthened its school of business administration, another continued to give degrees in forestry and nursing, while privately controlled universities in urban areas were as catholic in their offerings as any financed by the state. One element of the ancient four — professional education—had received nourishment from the combination of democracy and industrialization. It was forced to proliferate in a way to shock the admirers of the ancient stem. All manner of new vocations were assimilated within the sacred walls of a university, and graduates armed with special training in a variety of skills stood on the commencement platform as proudly as the future members of the clergy or the bar.

In short, in the course of seventy-five years or so the forces of democracy had taken the European idea of a university and transformed it. The American university today is as different from the nineteenth-century

British or Continental universities as the Renaissance universities of Italy and the Netherlands were different from those of the Middle Ages. Personally, I think the basic philosophy which almost unconsciously has shaped the growth of the modern American university is sound, for it is none other than a philosophy hostile to the supremacy of a few vocations; it is a philosophy moving toward the social equality of all useful labor.

As an offset to this increased emphasis on professional training (for I regard all university vocational education as a derivative of the ancient professions), there came about a strong movement to make American universities centers of scholarly work and scientific investigation. This movement was not only to some degree a counterbalance to the educational forces associated with the agricultural and mechanical colleges, but also a response to a challenge to make of some of the older institutions something more than advanced boarding schools for a special group.

In the middle of the last century the head of one of the Oxford colleges, an eminent scholar and educational reformer, saw no evidence that the university tradition had ever taken root in the United States. "America has no universities, as we understand the term," he wrote, "the institutions so-called being merely places for granting titular degrees." Taken literally this harsh judgment is undoubtedly false; yet it probably is not a gross exaggeration of the situation which then existed. The new spirit moving within the educational institutions of the country had not become evident to those outside our academic walls.

It was not until the Johns Hopkins University was opened at Baltimore that the idea of a university as a center of advanced learning came to have a prominent place in the public mind. It was not until Gilman had boldly proclaimed that "all departments of learning should be promoted" and that "the glory of the university should rest upon the character of the teachers and scholars . . . and not upon their number nor upon the buildings constructed for their use" — it was not until then that scholarship came into its own as part of the university tradition of the United States.

From this development, as we all know, came the growth of the graduate schools of arts and sciences, the introduction of new standards of excellence in regard to original work by scientists and scholars, and the growth of what is now sometimes referred to as the Ph.D. octopus. All this was slow at first but, like the other changes in the universities of America, gained speed during the period just before and just after the first World War. As a consequence, the American university has been in recent years something of a mental patient suffering from a schizophrenic disorder: on one day, or during one administration, the disciplines grouped under the banner of the arts, letters, and sciences represent the dominant personality; on another day, or during another administration, it is the vocational procession led by law and medicine that sweeps all before it.

But, as so often happens in the delightful chaos of American democracy, the various pressure groups to a large degree canceled out. [Looking back over the history of this century, we can see that the American universities drew strength from many different sources. The fact that the forces making for the new developments were not only often totally unrelated but at times apparently working one against another made little difference; the expansion and strengthening of the entire institution continued almost without interruption. The nature of the typical American university had emerged; whether any given institution was state-controlled or privately supported made little difference in the pattern] In some states there was a comprehensive system comprising several constituent members; in others all work was included in one academic institution.

As to the variety of the vocational training, one university or one university system might show considerable divergence from another; as to the strength of the faculties, there were, of course, wide differences; but as to their ideas of undergraduate education and their devotion to the welfare of the students, there was remarkable uniformity among them all. The significant fact was that no university which gave degrees in the ancient professions of medicine or law remained aloof from also giving degrees in such modern subjects as business administration, engineering, journalism, forestry, architecture, nursing, or education. And many were awarding the bachelor's degree for courses of study in vocational fields very distant, indeed, from the traditional disciplines of the arts and sciences.

To complete this brief and inadequate account of the Americanization of the university idea, it remains only to discuss general education as apart from vocational education. I have earlier referred to the "general education of the leading citizens" as one of those traditional elements in the university pattern which have remained constant through the centuries. A volume would be required to do justice to this aspect of the work of universities in different countries and in different periods of history. In a sense, this phase of university education is a by-product of the two main preoccupations of the scholars: the advancement of learning, and education for the professions — which includes, of course, the training of new scholars. In a sense, it is a by-product — yet a by-product which in the public eye (including the eye of future students) has often loomed as large as all the other functions of the university put together. And the larger it loomed the more emphasis we find put on student life, which has manifested itself in ways as different as the Oxford colleges, the German dueling clubs, and the American zest for intercollegiate athletics.

If we examine the role of the universities in the English-speaking countries in the seventeenth and eighteenth centuries, we find a fair proportion of the students preparing not for the church or the bar, but for public service or a career in letters. In England only slowly, in the Colonies more rapidly, the merchant families came to send their boys to a college or university in order to obtain the sort of general education required by the business positions they would later occupy. In terms of the total population, the number of young men who pursued this road, however, was small indeed. For the most part, only a special set of relatively wealthy families patronized the colleges and universities for this purpose; the poor boy entered only if he desired to become a scholar or a member of a learned profession.

The numbers were small in the eighteenth century and the first part of the nineteenth, because, except to those in the professions I have mentioned, the education thus acquired was of but little significance in later life. The same may be said of the situation throughout America as late as the middle of the last century. But then matters began to change. As part of the educational expansion more and more boys began to enter colleges and universities, not to study for the professions but for a general education as a preparation for later life in the business world. An acute observer reared in another culture might have seen at the turn of the century that American educational policy was steering American educational philosophy toward an ugly problem. As long as education beyond the high school was a matter for a very small fraction of the population and, except for learned and literary men, of no great moment in terms of subsequent success, it mattered little who went to college. But as more and more doors of opportunity in an increasingly industrialized society became closed to the non-college man, the question of who went to college raised new social and political problems. Today we are faced with the awkward questions raised in the beginning of this chapter: Have we real equality of educational opportunity at the college level? If not, what is the proper remedy? Is everyone to go to college?

Of one thing we can be sure — not everyone should have a professional training, even using this word in the broad American sense. This proposition requires no documentation. A second premise, almost equally obvious to those who are convinced of the validity of our American ideals, is that those who do obtain a professional education should be chosen on the basis of pure merit. This follows as a consequence of the doctrine of equality of educational opportunity which has been emphasized so frequently throughout this book. But it may be supported on entirely different grounds on the basis of the welfare of the nation. A modern industrialized, highly urbanized country can prosper only if the professions are full of capable, imaginative, and forward-looking men. We must have extremely able lawyers, doctors, teachers, scientists, and public servants. There is no place for nepotism in the recruitment of this corps of specialists. To the extent that we now fail to educate the potential talent of each generation, we are wasting one of the country's greatest assets. In the world today a highly industrialized nation simply cannot afford this type of waste. Yet no one familiar with the situation would deny that such a waste occurs.

In spite of the fact that America had remade the university and expanded the facilities for university students several fold, before the war there were many able youths to whom the professional world was barred. Evidence on this point has already been presented in Chapter 3, and it need not be repeated here. In the immediate postwar years, 1946–1948, thanks to the G. I. Bill, the universities and colleges have been crowded, and because of the large amount of Federal money expended, it is true that any adequately prepared veteran who wants a college education can obtain it. But when this war generation has been educated, what is then to come? Shall we revert to the prewar situation? Can we afford to do so either in terms of our ideals or our need for talent?

We must remember that as matters stand today the opportunities for professional education at low cost are very unequally and unfairly distributed in the United States. As was pointed out earlier, the urban family with a low income is in a relatively favored position since every city of any size has one or more universities (often tuition free). By living at home the student can receive professional training with only a small outlay in cash. On the other hand, those who grow up in smaller cities, towns, and rural areas are with rare exceptions beyond commuting distance to a university. For these young men and women, to attend an academic institution which gives professional training means living away from home with a consequent high expense. Clearly scholarships, loan funds, and opportunities for part-time work are the methods by which youths from rural areas must surmount the economic barriers which bar the road to the professions.

Since the major cost of advanced education, if the student is away from home, is board and lodging, one can argue that as far as possible the expansion of public education beyond high school should be arranged locally. Otherwise in order to offer equal opportunities we should have to envisage using public funds to provide years of free board and room for a considerable fraction of our high school graduates. But there are various types of professional and vocational education which can be given at only a few centers in even a very populous state. It is literally impossible, for example, to give adequate instruction in clinical medicine except in cities of sufficient size to support large hospitals. Similarly, advanced work in the arts, sciences, and letters can be done only where adequate libraries and laboratories are at hand. It is clearly in the national interest to find all the latent talent available for the lengthy training that research careers demand. Yet to establish research centers at every point in the United States where general education beyond the high school is desired would be not merely uneconomical, but impossible. The alternative, to strengthen our present universities and establish a national system of scholarships, seems the only answer. The way this might be done and how it might be financed will be the subject of the next chapter.

I venture to conclude this discussion of the universities by returning to my original proposition: the health of our universities depends on keeping a balance between the advancement of knowledge, professional education, general education, and the demands of student life. From time to time, every institution will be threatened by the overgrowth of one of these four elements or the atrophy of one or more. But by and large it seems clear that in the next few years it is the advancement of knowledge which will be in need of the greatest encouragement and support. I say this in spite of the present public concern with supporting research in the physical and biological sciences. I say it in part because of this concern. I am afraid that there will be so many research institutes founded by industry and philanthropy for very specific purposes that the university faculties will be drained dry of their productive men. Few laymen seem to realize the simple fact that it is men that count, and that first-rate investigators and original scholars are relatively rare phenomena and require long and careful training. That is why, to me, the spending of the taxpayers' money on a scholarship policy is fully as important as the establishment of a National Science Foundation to support basic research in our universities.

In a book about education there is no place for a long discussion of the role of the universities in advancing knowledge. I resist the temptation to explore many interesting and significant problems in this area. It is essential, however, to emphasize another aspect of the scholarly work of a university, one of great significance for the nation. I refer to intellectual, educational, and moral leadership — leadership not only of a state but of an entire section. This leadership of a community of scholars, like the leadership of an individual, requires, first, capacity based on expert knowledge; second, broad vision; third, courage. And of these the last is by no means the least significant. More and more I believe that the nation and different groups within the nation (geographic, social, or economic groups) must look to university scholars for guidance in handling basic social and economic problems.⌉ To this end the professors of these subjects must explore vigorously not only the fundamental aspects of man's behavior but the applications of our present knowledge.

One condition is essential: freedom of discussion, unmolested inquiry. As in the early days of this century, we must have a spirit of tolerance which allows the expression of a great variety of opinions. On this point there can be no compromise even in days of an armed truce. But we should be completely unrealistic if we failed to recognize the difficulties which arise from the ideological conflict which according to the premise of this book will be with us for years to come. Excited citizens are going to be increasingly alarmed about alleged "communist infiltration" into our schools and colleges. Reactionaries are going to use the tensions inherent in our armed truce as an excuse for attacking a wide group of radical ideas and even some which are in the middle of the road.

How are we to answer the thoughtful and troubled citizen who wonders if our universities are being used as centers for fifth column activities? By emphasizing again the central position in this country of tolerance of diversity of opinion and by expressing confidence that *our* philosophy is superior to all alien importations. After all, this is but one version of the far wider problem which we encounter at the outset: how are we to win the ideological conflict if it continues on a non-shooting basis? Clearly not by destroying our basic ideas but by strengthening them; clearly not by retreating in fear from the Communist doctrine but by going out vigorously to meet it. [Studying a philosophy does not mean endorsing it, much less proclaiming it. We study cancer in order to learn how to defeat it. We must study the Soviet philosophy in our universities for exactly the same reason. No one must be afraid to tackle that explosive subject before a class. If an avowed supporter of the Marx-Lenin-Stalin line can be found, force him into the open and tear his arguments to pieces with counter-arguments.] Some of the success of the Communist propaganda in this country before the war was due to the fact that it was like pornographic literature purveyed through an academic black market so to speak. For a certain type of youth this undercover kind of knowledge has a special attraction. And doctrines that are not combated in the classroom but treated merely with silence or contempt may be appealing to the immature.

The first requirement for maintaining a healthy attitude in our universities in these days, therefore, is to get the discussion of modern Marxism out into the open. The second is to recognize that we are not at peace but in a period of an armed truce. That means that the activities which go with war, such as vigorous secret intelligence, sabotage, and even planned disruption of the basic philosophy of a nation may well proceed. We must be on our guard. We must be realistic about the activities of agents of foreign powers, but at the same time be courageous in our support of the basis of our own creed, the maximum of individual freedom. We should be certain that any steps we take to counteract the work of foreign agents within our borders do not damage irreparably the very fabric we seek to save. The government, of course, must see to it that those who are employed in positions of responsibility and trust are persons of intelligence, discretion, and unswerving loyalty to the national interest. But in disqualifying others we should proceed with the greatest caution. Certain men and women who temperamentally are unsuited for employment by a Federal agency none the less can serve the nation in other ways. They may be entitled to our full respect as citizens though we may disagree with their opinions. For example, a person whose religious beliefs make him a conscientious objector is automatically disqualified from employment by the nation in matters pertaining to the use of force or preparation for the use of force. On the other hand, such a man may be an intellectual and moral leader of the greatest importance for the welfare of our society.

These obvious considerations have bearing on the problems of staffing a university. Universities, however they may be financed or controlled, are neither government bureaus nor private corporations; the professors are not hired employees. The criteria for joining a community of scholars are in some ways unique. They are not to be confused with the requirements of a Federal bureau. For example, I can imagine a naïve scientist or a philosopher with strong loyalties to the advancement of civilization and the unity of the world who would be a questionable asset to a government department charged with negotiations with other nations; the same man because of his professional competence might be extremely valuable to a university. Such conclusions are obvious to anyone who takes the trouble to think carefully about the degrees of prudence and sophistication met with in human beings. Such considerations will be self-evident to all who analyze the complex problem of loyalty.

The third condition necessary for maintaining free inquiry within our universities is to ask the scholars themselves to declare their own basic social philosophy. We must then be prepared in our universities to be sure that we have a variety of views represented and that in the classroom our teachers be careful scholars rather than propagandists. But the unpopular view must be protected for we would be quite naïve to imagine that there are no reactionaries who would like to drive all liberals from the halls of learning. This issue arises, of course, not in the physical sciences but in connection with the social sciences and sometimes the humanities.

The statement is often made that science is neutral as far as value judgments are concerned. This is one of those three-quarter truths fully as dangerous as half-truths. Let us consider the medical sciences today. Investigators and practitioners concerned with human disease almost unconsciously accept a set of values which limits their activity and also serves as a powerful spur to their endeavors. This fact seems to be overlooked when the neutrality of science is proclaimed. Much more than the Hippocratic oath is involved. Only in a society where life is considered preferable to death and where health is glorified would funds flow freely for the study of disease. Only where the sanctity of each individual is so strongly felt that it is regarded as a paramount duty to save every life possible at whatever cost would physicians, surgeons, and medical scientists act as they do today. Our standard of medical care and our desire to raise it is based on a series of value judgments. Let me make it plain — I am not questioning the assumptions. I am merely pointing to the existence of these postulates basic to all work in the medical sciences. I do so because I believe the situation is analogous in the case of those scholars who are studying human behavior and human relations; but the analogy has not yet been fully realized.

The assumptions of the medical men and their allies

are by now fairly well accepted in modern industrialized nations, though in practice the value placed on human life certainly is subject to wide variations. The assumptions essential for the proper functioning of the political scientist, economist, psychologist, anthropologist, and sociologist in our unique society, however, are, I believe, as special as the history of this society itself. The equivalent of the Hippocratic oath which these men might well formulate to make their biases explicit would therefore be related closely to the type of society in which they propose to operate. Even the English and the American versions might vary at several points, but the essentials would be the same. Totalitarian nations, however, would use the techniques developed by these scientists for very different ends; and their use would condition the further advancement of the sciences themselves. Powerful tools are in the process of being forged by the scientists who study man as a social animal. These tools can be used to further or to destroy certain types of behavior and certain social patterns. It is essential for the men themselves to clarify in their own minds their own standards of value in many matters, just as, long ago, the medical profession took a definite stand on the issues confronting those whose knowledge includes the key to the life or death of an individual in distress.

A study of the writings of the last fifty years makes it evident that the myth of the neutrality of science has been used as a smoke screen for reactionaries and radicals alike. For example, within recent times some who

wished to see a tight class structure develop in the
United States have analyzed society in so-called scien
tific terms. Likewise, those who wished for a socialistic
state can quote the results of modern investigators of
society for their own ends. My objection to these procedures stems less from my lack of enthusiasm for the
objectives than from the failure of the authors to be
explicit as to their premises. Gunnar Myrdal has faced
this question squarely and said: "There is no other
device for excluding biases in social science than to face
the valuations and to introduce them as explicitly stated,
specific and sufficiently concretized value premises."

I am inclined to think that, to forward their own
work, scholars and practitioners concerned with the sciences of man might well join together and issue a proc-
lamation. Or if that is too much to hope for, recognizing the importance of rugged independence among
learned men, each one might make his own individual
position clear.

Those who worry about radicalism in our schools and
colleges are often either reactionaries who themselves
do not bear allegiance to the traditional American principles or defeatists who despair of the success of our
own philosophy in an open competition. The first group
are consciously or unconsciously aiming at a transformation of this society, perhaps initially not as revolutionary
or violent as that which the Soviet agents envisage, but
one eventually equally divergent from our historic goals.
The others are unduly timid about the outcome of a

battle of *ideas*; they lack confidence in our own intellectual armament. (I mean literally the battle of ideas
not espionage or sabotage by secret agents.) They often
fail to recognize that diversity of opinion within the
framework of loyalty to our free society is not only basic
to a university but to the entire nation. For in a democracy with our traditions only those reasoned convictions
which emerge from diversity of opinion can lead to that
unity and national solidarity so essential for the welfare
of our country — essential not only for our own security
but even more a requisite for intelligent action toward
the end we all desire, namely, the conversion of the present armed truce into a firm and lasting peace.

Like all other democratic institutions based on the
principles of toleration, individual freedom, and the
efficacy of rational methods, the universities are certain
to meet with many difficulties as they seek to preserve
their integrity during this period of warring ideologies.
But we would do well to remember this is not the first
time that communities of scholars have been disturbed
by doctrinal quarrels so deep-seated as to be in the
nature of smoldering wars. The history of Oxford and
Cambridge during the Civil Wars of the seventeenth
century is interesting reading on this point. At that
time the "true friends of learning" rallied to the support
of those ancient institutions and protected them against
the excesses of both sides. Today, likewise, the friends
of learning must recognize the dangers which might
threaten the universities if tempers rise as the armed

truce lengthens. They must seek to increase the number of citizens who understand the true nature of universities, the vital importance of the tradition of free inquiry, the significance of life tenure for the older members of each faculty, the fact that violent differences of opinion are essential for education. They must be realistic about the fanatic followers of the Soviet philosophy who seek to infiltrate, control, and disrupt democratic organizations including student clubs. But they must also recognize the threat that comes from those reactionaries who are ready if a wave of hysteria should mount to purge the institutions of all doctrines contrary to their views. In short, our citadels of learning must be guarded by devoted laymen in all walks of life who realize the relation between education and American democracy. So protected, the universities need not worry unduly about infiltration of Marxist subversive elements or intimidation from without. They will remain secure fortresses of our liberties.

10

LOWERING THE ECONOMIC BARRIERS

The report of the President's Commission on Higher Education dated December 1947 recommended that:

The American people should set as their ultimate goal an educational system in which at no level — high school, college, graduate school or professional school — will a qualified individual in any part of the country encounter an insuperable economic barrier to the attainment of the kind of education suited to his aptitudes and interests.

With this general statement of the doctrine of equality of educational opportunity no one who accepts the basic tenets of our American democratic faith can possibly disagree. When it comes to a formulation of the ways and means of lowering the present economic barriers, however, there is ample ground for disagreement even among the most enthusiastic supporters of public education. Take the question of the professions, for example. No one can doubt that before the war many boys and girls who, if properly educated, would have become leaders of professions did not proceed with their advanced education. In part this was the failure of our elementary and secondary schools which to a large degree has been a consequence of inadequate financial support. This failure is clearly one type of economic barrier, for relatively well-to-do parents may send their boys and girls to private schools and thus prepare them for eventual professional education.

The second type of economic barrier is the cost of education beyond the high school which is largely the expense of being away from home. As previously stated, there are two ways of lowering this economic barrier to advanced education: one is to provide advanced training locally, the other to offer scholarships to enable a student to go to a college or university beyond commuting distance from his or her home. In terms merely of keeping the expenditures at a minimum, local education seems the answer. But, as was made evident in the preceding chapter, a center for professional training cannot be located at every crossroad. The number of universities in any region of the country must be relatively few. On the other hand, two years of general education and vocational education can be provided almost as readily as the last two years of high school. Therefore, this type of advanced education lends itself to development in every city and almost every large-sized town. This being the case, in every discussion of equalizing opportunity it is important to distinguish between (a) improving the elementary and secondary schools, (b) providing for general and vocational education locally, and (c) enabling our professions to recruit from the ablest youth irrespective of considerations of geography or family finances.

The three phases of the basic problem have one thing

in common: they require a very large increase in expenditure of public funds. And since citizens are also taxpayers, it is at this point that disagreement usually enters. Whose taxes are going to be increased to foot the bill? Is local, state, or Federal money going to be involved? Before answering these crucial questions we must first explore the basic problem of the relation of our schools and colleges to our governmental structure. This may seem a dull subject, but failure to analyze this matter carefully has been responsible for much futile discussion about the costs of improving our education.

Let us start with the elementary and secondary schools. These institutions are firmly rooted historically in the local community. In spite of a considerable diversity in the development of universal education in the different states, I think it safe to say that the doctrine of local control of the school is one of the beliefs ingrained in the American mind. The connection of this idea with our general theory of the relation of the individual to organized society is evident. Perhaps it springs from a pioneer reluctance to admit the validity of any control by a government official who is not a local personage subject to removal by those who temporarily gave him power. Whatever historians or political theorists may say, the implicit assumption of the average citizen about his school involves the fundamental notion of local control. As far as possible the school should be the direct responsibility of the local people. Only thus can the school serve the community;

furthermore, in a nation with great geographic diversity only by adherence to this idea can we have a harmonious development of public education. So far, so good; even the most cautious taxpayer and the most conservative supporter of public schools will subscribe to these premises.

The constitutional unit on matters of education, however, is not the town or city, but the state. This fact may be a jolt to some readers, but is obviously a consequence of the nature of our Federal structure. In each one of the forty-eight states of the Union, public education is organized by laws and the state constitution. The degree of supervision of the activities of the local communities in school matters varies enormously from state to state. By and large one may say that the basic notion of the maximum of local control has been adhered to by a delegation of authority: the state has given to the local government or school district the power to raise money to support the schools through taxes primarily on real estate. The sovereign state has likewise granted to local groups the power to elect officials to run the school. Generalizing over a wide and uncertain area, one may say that to the degree that local taxes can support the schools in any given state, the relation of the local school to the state government is tenuous. In recent years, however, it has become more and more evident that the taxing base of the local community is not broad enough to support the type of school required by our modern society. Even in some of the older and more conservative states

it is becoming increasingly clear that the taxing power of
the state as such must be invoked in order to provide sufficient funds for the local schools in many cities, towns
and rural areas. The relative amount of money raised by
state taxes and allocated to local schools varies enormously; in a few states it is as low at 15% of the total
school expenditures, and in at least one as high as 90%.
The proper percentage depends entirely on the situation
in the state in question.

The rational method of handling this whole complicated subject of the source of taxes for public schools
would seem to be as follows: the legislature should set
the standards for all the public schools in the state in
general terms and determine a sound program for jointly
financing schools through a combination of state and
local taxes. The legislature must also determine the fair
share in terms of local tax rates which each district will
contribute. All local units should be encouraged to support schools beyond the minimum established throughout the state to the extent of their willingness to use
their own tax resources for this purpose. Of course,
history, traditions, and politics prevent in every state
any simplified and logical approach to a complex matter.
For one cannot consider raising money for schools without bringing in the whole problem of taxation.

Curiously enough there is relatively little interest in
this whole question of the relation of the state to the
school in many sections of the country where the tradition of local autonomy is strong. Local taxpayers' asso-

ciations, which at times have been rather hostile critics of the public schools, often assume that the *status quo* must continue as regards the allocation of taxes; assuming that the local real estate must carry the burden, they sometimes argue only in terms of the effect of school expenditures on the local taxes, ignoring the broader issue of increasing state aid. To be sure, the number of different systems in effect throughout the United States is so great and the details so confusing that no clear-cut issue can be dramatized on a national scale. As a consequence, probably not one civic-minded citizen in ten knows how the schools in his town or city are financed or what state laws affect the operations.

There is no question, of course, but that the entire state as the sovereign body has a responsibility for all the schools. We have always been a mobile people in geographic terms, and are perhaps more so today than ever before. The boy or girl being educated in a rural school is a future citizen of the state, not just a resident of an isolated village. This is the reason why state funds must increasingly flow to the local schools. This is the reason why the state educational authorities must take a certain degree of responsibility in all school matters. The ideal relationship between the statehouse and the town or city or school district should be not one of control or supervision but of intelligent and broad leadership. There are examples of sound practice in this regard in the United States, and other cases where the situation could and should be improved. A critical comparative study of the relation of the state to the public local school in each of the forty-eight states would be illuminating. Perhaps some citizens' committee or a national group will sponsor the writing of such a document for laymen. If so, it should be put in the hands of all leaders of the nation.

We are now ready to tackle the thorny question of Federal aid. Here the disagreement is apt to become violent indeed. But I submit, an analysis of the question of state aid is a prerequisite to an intelligent discussion of this highly controversial topic. Federal aid to the states to assist elementary and secondary education is but the logical extension of state aid for local schools. Federal funds are a necessity in those states where extending the tax base to the state still fails to provide adequate support for the elementary and secondary schools. The fact of the matter is that the resources of certain of our states are simply insufficient to finance the type of school our society requires in the mid-twentieth century. And everyone who has doubts about the principle of Federal aid for our elementary and secondary schools must recall that in every state we are educating future citizens of the entire nation. This is the answer to the question often heard — why should the residents of the wealthy states be taxed by the Federal government to supply funds for the education of children in the poorer states? The reply is that the future citizens of a wealthy state, perhaps of a rich city, are being educated right now in some of the economically backward states, and their education is shockingly inadequate in many instances.

Few challenge the statement that the schools in certain sections of this country are very poor, largely because of the small amount of money expended. In a great number of rural areas, towns, and even cities our public schools are far below any reasonable standard. The proponents of Federal aid readily concede that to some degree this gross inadequacy, reflected in the salaries of the teachers, is due to the failure of the state itself to do its share; in some instances it is the result of corrupt politics; but in at least a dozen states the basic cause is the lack of taxable resources in the state itself. The opponents of Federal aid have a hard time denying this proposition.

The figures presented before the Congressional committees considering legislation on this subject since the war show conclusively that some states do not have the resources to provide a satisfactory education from either local or state taxes. For example, one may examine the expenditure per child in average daily attendance and the percentage of the income in the state spent for schools. In 1944–45, thirty states spent for public schools from 1.5 to 2.6 per cent of the total income of their citizens (a figure which is calculated as is the national income and a measure of the state's potential capacity to raise funds by rigorous taxation). Yet in that group of states we find New Jersey by expending 1.74 per cent of its people's income provided $198 per child in school, while North Carolina by expending 1.91 per cent raised only $69 per child in school. And Mississippi provided only $45 per child in school by using 1.64 per cent of its citizens' total income. While few would deny that almost every state should spend a greater per cent of its income for schools, it is clear that in not a few states even raising the figure to the average of the highest half dozen states (2.38 per cent) would still leave a very low figure for the expenditure per child. Thus, in North Carolina 2.38 per cent of the total income of the state's inhabitants in 1945 would have provided $86, and in Mississippi only $65 per child. Compare these figures with the $127 or more per pupil spent in 1944–45 by over half of the states. (Note the figures are per child in school. They are based on the average daily attendance. The average spent per child in each state would be smaller, for in some states many children of school age are not in school.)

The ideal pattern of state aid places the maximum responsibility on the local community; this responsibility means local control and likewise a high local tax rate. The ideal pattern for Federal aid should involve the flow of funds only to those states which have already demonstrated that they have done their utmost from their own resources, and where in spite of the state's effort the funds available per pupil are below a minimum figure. (Detailed formulas for making some such criteria effective were carefully worked out as a basis for the legislation sponsored in 1947–48 by Senator Taft.) Just as the state taxing power should supplement but not supplant a high local tax for local schools, so, too, the Federal taxing power should be a supplement to state and local support. The Federal government should provide additional assistance only to those states which require aid to raise education to a minimum standard, and which have clearly demonstrated their willingness to tax themselves to the limit for this purpose.

Federal control is potentially far more dangerous than state control. Indeed, the dangers in this quarter loom so large in some people's minds that they are opposed to all Federal aid. This attitude is one I understand but with which I heartily disagree; on the one hand it fails to appreciate the real need, and on the other is too defeatist about the nature of our democracy. Granted a sufficient number of wide-awake citizens with a *national* interest in public education to act as watch dogs on Congress, we need not be too apprehensive about educational bureaucracies or centralized control. Admittedly we must arouse far greater interest in the welfare of education among our people. But powerful political pressures already exist which guarantee that a stiff fight will always be waged for a decentralized school system. School administrators and school teachers are almost unanimous in their vigorous insistence on the doctrine of local control of education, and they are well organized and well led. As long as their voice is heard (and it will be), I have little fear that Federal funds granted to the states for the use of public schools will lead to Federal control of our local education.

There is one aspect of this problem that is not at first apparent, and yet which is of prime importance. Federal funds should flow to the *state* and be dispersed within the state by state authorities acting according to state law. If this principle is adhered to in any plan for Federal aid to schools, control of education from Washington by the most zealous bureaucrat will be almost impossible to achieve. Let it be noted carefully that the points of contact, so to speak, would be kept to forty-eight; no Federal agents would be involved at the school level. Federal funds would be merged with state funds; thus the problem of Federal control merges with the problem of state control, always an issue before the voters.

A bit of history is important in this connection. We have had some experiences with the use of Federal funds spent *locally by Federal administrators* for educational purposes. In the thirties we saw the growth of something approaching a system of Federal vocational schools throughout the country. This was the outgrowth of the vast expenditure of Federal money for relief. Without entering into any argument about the necessity for this program or the general pattern of the administration of such relief, one may say categorically that the educational implications were most serious. A competition developed between schools inadequately financed but locally controlled and parallel institutions amply supplied from Washington and controlled from Washington. The prospects were not pleasant for those who see the necessity for community responsibility for education. The lessons of this period should not be forgotten. If our well-established public schools founded on the doctrine of a high degree of local autonomy are properly supported, there will be no subsequent temptation to repeat this experiment. The pattern will be set for Federal expenditures for school purposes on an indirect, not a direct, basis.

One may hope that if a proper pattern be established, certain practices now in existence can be altered. Over the years there has grown up a piecemeal approach to the whole problem of spending Federal money for education. Congress now votes funds to be expended in our schools for special purposes such as vocational training and school lunches. A review of this whole situation is badly needed; some of the expenditures should be eliminated and others coördinated and fitted into a sound scheme of administration. Washington should deal with state authorities, not with the local schools; Federal agents should be conspicuous by their absence.

Before leaving the whole subject of the support of the elementary and secondary schools, it is worth reiterating the obvious fact that in some areas in almost every state and in almost every area in certain states, the inadequacies of the schools constitute the chief barrier to advanced education. Finding a proper tax base for the schools (local, state, and where necessary Federal) is an essential step in lowering the economic barriers to education. We focus attention too much, perhaps, on the transition from high school to college and often fail to realize how much talent is lost because of the insufficient public support of many of our secondary schools. To be sure, those with sufficient income in some localities can bypass inadequate public schools by sending the children to private schools. And this is done to an alarming extent throughout the urban centers of the nation — more so than a generation or two ago. That this practice represents a retreat from our goal of equality of opportunity and thus diminishes our national solidarity needs no emphasis. Our free elementary and secondary schools should be the first concern of all thoughtful believers in American democracy. The first call on Federal money should be at this crucial point.

We are now in a position to consider the removal of the second economic barrier by providing free education beyond the high school on a vastly expanded scale. Here we must at once recognize that our ambitions must be limited; all that we can reasonably hope is to show real progress every decade toward the goal of equality of opportunity. No educational reforms can be put into operation overnight, particularly when we consider social as well as economic barriers; prejudice is deep-seated and only slowly can be eliminated by education. We must recognize the necessity of evolution rather than revolution in this field of equalizing advanced education. We have a diversity of colleges and universities in this country that must seem a chaotic nightmare to a foreign visitor. Almost every institution of any age has its roots deep in some local community or some social or religious group. Perhaps some of the colleges may have outlived their usefulness in their present form, but the process of transformation will be slow; in the case of the privately supported ones this is particularly true.

The line between private and public institutions is hazy when we come to universities. While the private secondary school is only a specialized competitor with the public high school, many privately endowed colleges and universities can claim to be *national* institutions. As far as methods of lowering the economic barriers to the professions are at issue, the two types of universities may be considered together. For even if the state supports its university so generously that no fees are charged, the student still has large expenses for room and board unless he happens to live in the college town. I remind the reader once again of the fact already mentioned that almost every large city has one or more universities. Therefore, the need for lowering of the economic barriers to the professions primarily relates to children of low income families in small cities, towns, and rural areas. Scholarship assistance on a generous scale is needed for the gifted youths from these localities.

A scholarship program looking toward equalizing the opportunity to enter a profession might be financed on the basis of private philanthropy, state funds, and Federal funds. Before the war the first two sources were being tapped; with the passage of the so-called G. I. Bill a vast Federal scholarship program was instituted. Before many years have passed the veterans will have left the colleges and professional schools and we shall revert to the prewar status. There has been agitation to establish a Federal scholarship system on a permanent basis, not unlike that for veterans of World War II. There can be no doubt that in terms of equalizing opportunity the G. I. Bill was a revolutionary forward step. If so, some may argue, why should it not be continued? This method of distributing taxpayers' money to all types of colleges and universities (private and public alike) has not led to any trace of Federal control, so let us finance advanced education on this basis, one may plausibly contend.

There are a number of difficulties that have to be considered before any such sweeping proposal can be endorsed. First, there is the very practical matter of expense; second is the old problem of the tax base (why Federal rather than state support of scholarships); the third involves the wisdom of a wholesale indiscriminate national scholarship program. The last consideration is by far the most important, and the one on which students of the subject are in rather strenuous disagreement. For example, the President's Commission on Higher Education advocates the immediate passage of legislation by Congress of a "national program of scholarships to be administered by the States in accordance with general standards established by the Federal government." By 1953 the appropriations (initially to be $120,000,000) would be increased in an amount "sufficient to provide scholarships for twenty per cent of the non-veteran enrollment." In addition a fellowship program for 30,000 students by 1953 is recommended to encourage "youth of special talent to rise to the top level in the professions, research and instruction," such fellowships to be provided by the Federal government at an annual cost of $45,000,000. These recommendations taken together with the Commission's belief that the enrollment in the "graduate and professional schools" should be increased 170 per cent seem to some of us to represent much too ambitious a program for the immediate future.

While heartily endorsing the basic principles of the recommendations, I for one feel that the Commission is attempting to make haste too rapidly. Furthermore, I believe a sounder program would result from a greater emphasis on the distinction between professional education on the one hand, and general and vocational education on the other. We are in a period of experimentation as regards the expansion of post-high-school facilities; in order to obtain an efficient expenditure of the taxpayers' money, we must as far as possible provide education locally. Furthermore, the line between university work and college work is still far from sharp, and it is by no means clear that we need as great an expansion of the four-year institutions as the Commission recommends. I am willing to assume the correctness of their statement that "at least thirty-two per cent of our population has the mental ability to complete an advanced liberal or specialized professional education." (This is based on their study of the results of the Army Classification Test during the war.) I feel quite sure, however, that the subsequent professional performance of the top 20 per cent of this group (6 per cent of the age group) would be of a very different quality from that of the bottom half. The immediate objective might well be not an increase in numbers but the recruiting of better students. The composition of our prewar student body in the professional courses was to a large degree accidental; as the Commission clearly demonstrates, reasons of geography and birth played far too large a role. We should plan to recruit a vastly superior group of young men and women in the professions by a scholarship policy, but we might well proceed at the start by taking a few professions at a time and aiming at high quality rather than numbers.

Specifically, I would advocate beginning with a Federal scholarship program for youth headed for the professions of medicine, dentistry, public health, and research careers in the sciences. This group of professions is clearly of prime interest to the entire nation. One can argue that all professions transcend state boundaries. But the national significance of having first-rate men in the callings just enumerated is beyond doubt or cavil. Eventually all the professions might be included in a Federally financed program, but the chances of obtaining favorable action by Congress would seem to be greatly increased by keeping the first step relatively short. Also, it would be well initially to apply the system to those professions where potential talent is relatively easy to discover at an early age. As I envisage the plan, the students receiving a Federal scholarship would be selected on graduation from high school on the basis of a nation-wide examination. As in the case with the veterans today, the holder of the scholarship would choose his own university.

I may be overcautious in this approach and too insistent that the success of a scholarship program be appraised before it is expanded. But there is no more reason to waste public money in this area than anywhere else. My chief worry, however, comes from a fear that we may educate more doctors, lawyers, engineers, scientists, college professors than our economy can support. It has happened in the past, though not in the United States. There was serious unemployment in the learned professions in Germany between the two World Wars. There might be a similar unemployment in this nation even at a time of prosperity if we fail to diversify our post-high-school education. No one can do more than sound a warning; the facts are not available to warrant a firm conclusion. It will take a more exhaustive survey of the national scene than has yet been made to enable us to arrive at the first approximation of the number that should be trained for each profession. The importance of such a study is clear and might well be undertaken by the Federal government. The enrollment in our professional schools could then be adjusted within limits every decade and something approaching a reasonable assurance given to the graduates that their training was not in vain.

"But why worry?" the reader may be inclined to ask. "What harm does it do if a man is trained to be a lawyer, architect, doctor, philosopher, or chemist, and then can't find professional employment? He can always run a filling station or work on an assembly line and will be a better citizen because of the advanced education he has received." This is an intriguing argument and by no means rare. But is the basic premise right? May not advanced specialized education which leads nowhere make a man a desperately unhappy citizen and hence an unstable member of the body politic? It is a rare individual who is not deeply frustrated if he has spent years in acquiring certain skills and knowledge and then finds society unable to find a place for him to function according to his expectations; and from frustrated individuals with long education and considerable intelligence society has much to fear. From such people come the leaders of anti-democratic movements whether they originate from the right or left. It is both cruel and unwise as well as wasteful to operate a public educational system that produces many of this sort. The wisest and fairest course would seem to be to graduate somewhat too few rather than too many from our universities in any given year.

Finally we come to the matter of financing the expansion of the local two-year terminal colleges which have already been referred to several times in the last few chapters. Those institutions which are now coming to be called "community colleges" offer the best hope of meeting the postwar surge for vast expansion of education beyond the high school. They likewise can serve most effectively as centers for adult education. Their curricula should combine general education and vocational training, and they should be defined as terminal two-year colleges. By and large, the educational road should fork at the end of the high school; though an occasional transfer of a student from a two-year college to a university should not be barred. By improving our guidance program in the schools, the professional talent can be found at an early age, and by providing adequate scholarships this talent can be sent to the universities for the four, five, six, or seven years of professional education that are required.

The movement to establish more two-year free colleges locally has been gaining ground in the last few years. For these colleges to fulfill the desired function, however, will require genuine public support, not merely the educators' blessing. But before such support is forthcoming, there will have to be a rather complete change in public opinion. By and large, people think of colleges as four-year colleges or universities. The new status of a local two-year institution will require careful and repeated explanation in many states. Above all, the new institutions will have to be made as attractive as possible; if they are merely the colleges for the discards from other institutions, they will surely not succeed.

I believe that the two-year community colleges should be authorized to grant a bachelor's degree. This is the badge of respectability for most Americans; indeed, the letters have almost mystical significance in the United States. To give the same degree as the four-year college (the A.B. or B.S.) would merely be confusing to all concerned. But a two-year degree of bachelor of general studies (B.G.S.) might well represent the final degree for a majority of college students. More important than degrees is the type of education and social life. These colleges should provide general education and vocational training of various types to accommodate a spread of interests and aptitudes among the students. There is no reason why the course thus offered — a combination of job training and education for a full life of civic responsibility — might not be superior to that provided in many a liberal arts curriculum in a large and crowded university.

Those of us who believe the two-year community colleges are a significant step forward in the march toward our goal of equalizing educational opportunity have high hopes that they will prosper in every state. But we realize that such colleges first must be accepted by the leading citizens of each locality, particularly by managers of industry. The present emphasis by employers on the importance of a degree from a four-year college could be quite disastrous if continued — disastrous, that is, for the development of the new educational picture in which the two-year college plays so significant a role. Admittedly the adjustment of the community to the idea of the respectability of a two-year college will be a slow process, particularly in certain states; but if the case is put up squarely to the taxpayers I believe the issue will be understood. Businessmen will then gradually come to judge applicants for "white-collar" positions less in terms of the length of the college course; they will regard a two-year degree as adequate education for the first step on the competitive ladder. They will show their faith in these new institutions by enrolling their own sons and daughters, reserving the four-year college for those who have professional ambitions and the requisite capacity for "book learning." At present many of our leading four-year colleges are in effect the first step in the professional journey; more than half of the graduates of a number of these institutions go on to universities for professional work. I am inclined to think that in the next few years the percentage will and should increase. There will always be some students, of course, who decide that four years of a liberal arts college are sufficient and enter business life directly on graduation. This is inevitable under any system; even in the professional schools there always will be some who drop out at every stage.

To accommodate the proper expansion of education

beyond the high school, a very large increase of expenditures by the states and local communities for these community colleges will be required. What should be the pattern for the participation of the Federal government in this urgent educational matter? Exactly the same as that required for the effective operation of the public elementary and secondary schools. The local community should bear its share of the expense and should control these community colleges; the state should assist when needed (and this will be in most instances) and exercise leadership and some supervision. Federal funds should flow to those states which are doing their utmost to promote this expansion of post-high-school education and according to the need. If this pattern is established, one need not fear Federal control at this stage of education any more than at the lower levels. Without the use of the taxing power of the Federal government, however, there can be no adequate expansion of community colleges in many sections of the country.

To what extent should state and Federal money be used to expand the four-year state university (or universities) as well as to promote local two-year colleges? This and similar problems must be left to each state to determine; a generalization applicable to the whole nation is impossible. In the opinion of more than one administrator of a state university, the pressure of numbers on those institutions in these postwar years has reached a serious point. Where this is true, the urgent need of terminal two-year colleges seems evident. No one can be more eloquent as to the necessity for providing advanced education locally (through community colleges) than those who are responsible for the state universities with their tremendously expanded student bodies. To some degree all *American* universities provide general education, for the historical reasons outlined in the previous chapter. Those located in large urban areas must function both as community colleges and universities. This adds a complication and by itself prevents any nation-wide generalization. But by and large the chance that a given university can fulfil its prime function as a center for professional education and the advancement of knowledge rests on the expansion of other types of colleges to provide for the large numbers demanding general and vocational training beyond the high school stage.

Now if the citizen interested in public education has been able to survive this somewhat technical discussion of ways and means of spending money to improve our schools, I trust he will be willing to read a few words more about the all-important subject of guidance or counseling. For it has been well said that really effective counseling is the keystone of the arch of a widespread educational system dedicated to the principle of equality of opportunity. A democracy, unlike a totalitarian state, cannot force its youth into what the authorities consider the appropriate groove of advanced education. In this republic of free men, no official can decree what line of study must be pursued. Though public opinion might well be aware of the fact that the number of doctors should be greatly increased, yet the state is powerless (and should be) to order the most promising youths with scientific talent into the study of medicine. There is even a strong popular feeling of resentment against any tendency of educational authorities to limit the number of boys and girls who study any given subject. Any idea of telling them what they must study of a specialized nature would be thrown out of court by the American public without a hearing.

Yet, if we consider a thousand boys and girls, we all know how wide is the spread of ability among them and how varied are the talents. For the welfare of youth as well as for the welfare of the country, the varied talents should be developed in different ways. Some individuals in this group, to find their most useful and satisfying place, need but little formal education beyond high school. Some, however, should have many further years of intensive training.

How is the sorting out process to be accomplished? The answer is by the democratic method of enlightenment and pursuasion. To quote from *Education for All American Youth*:

the keystone of the school program is guidance — personal assistance to individual boys and girls in making their plans and decisions about careers, education, employment, and all sorts of personal problems.

Guidance is no mechanical process, whereby counselors and teachers sort out boys and girls as a grading machine sorts apples. . . . Guidance is rather the high art of helping boys and girls to plan their own actions wisely, in the full light of all the facts that can be mustered about themselves and about the world in which they work and live. . . . Important new factors enter into guidance as boys and girls move into the later teens. During the years just ahead, most of these youth will make plans and decisions with far-reaching effects on their lives. They will have to decide what occupations they are going to enter; whether they will stay in the . . . district or move away; what education they want and where to get it; when to go to work, where, and at what jobs; whether to marry soon or wait a few years; and so on. For each decision, plans must be formulated and carried out.

All discussion of scholarship programs and guidance of gifted youth into professional channels must recognize the inertia of public opinion on educational matters. The average citizen has been very loath until recently to admit the reality of talent. His views are reflected in the press and by his elected representatives. Only in matters connected with organized sport does the average American think clearly and realistically about the significance of innate ability. Countless parents condemn schools, colleges, and universities because their offspring are not being transformed into doctors and lawyers of great promise; but very few condemn the athletic director and his coaches because a son fails to develop into an All-American football player; and fewer still expect the college to make even an average athlete out of a frail and badly coördinated youth. Yet when it comes to studies, parents and children often expect the school and college to accomplish the equivalent of turning a cripple into a football player. And for this attitude the educational fraternity must take its share of blame. Every teacher worth his or her salt has to take a roseate view both of the potentialities of the pupils and the transforming power of education. Friends and supporters of various schools and colleges, who in this century have been seeking either more public funds, or more students, or more gifts (or all three), have quite consciously fostered the idea that education can work miracles. As a result of all this muddy thinking, the reality of talent is all too often denied by the average American citizen.

What has been called the "Jacksonian tradition" in American thinking, combined with the propaganda of certain educators, has spread the idea that any American child can, if he wants, with the aid of proper education, become anything he desires. The very fact that so-called higher education, particularly in the institutions with the highest standards and greatest reputation, has been available to a large degree only to the children of the upper income groups has made suspect the whole process of professional education. By denying the reality of intellectual talent, the "Jacksonian democrat" can also minimize the significance of professional training. Neither "brains" nor wealth determines which men get ahead in this American democracy, he declares; the only thing that counts, this sturdy individualist would maintain, is will power. And in spite of the historic connection between the mores of the U.S.A.

and the doctrine of predestination, most Americans are quite convinced that each man's will is free.

We meet here a social phenomenon of great interest and one that has played an important role in the development of the United States. One of the most baffling experiences for a foreigner is to encounter this strain in our thinking; it seems to him the democracy of the "levelers" of three centuries ago; it seems equalitarianism gone wild. To assume that the graduate of a night law school is just as well trained as one who has won honors at a famous university school of law seems to a foreign scholar either ludicrous or disastrous. Yet, while admitting that this American blindness to differences in ability and training along professional lines has worked much evil in the past, I believe it has been a healthy symptom of the vitality of our democratic life. Such leveling doctrines were the antibodies supplied unconsciously by the body politic to counteract the claims of those who had enjoyed "the privileges of a higher education." Here we have one of the instinctive defense mechanisms of American democracy at work to guard against the ascendancy of a privileged group.

There may be some who think I am stretching a long bow in thus ascribing to the American electorate a prejudice against high standards of professional training, and breaking the bow perhaps in relating this prejudice to a general social and political philosophy. If so, I only ask the skeptics to try to persuade a legislative group in Washington or in a number of state capitols as to the desirability of finding intellectual talent and educating this talent at government expense. I ask the same skeptics to look at the recorded debates on the state approval of medical schools with inadequate staffs and low standards. The fact that so many of our elected representatives are lawyers has had an important bearing on educational legislation. Because some men of great native ability have been successful in the practice of law even on the basis of very poor preparation, the false conclusion has been drawn that law schools with high standards are either unimportant or a positive evil. And by analogy the same argument has been advanced regarding medical and scientific training.

Clearly the remedy for the evil which has evoked this democratic defense response — the evil of inequality of educational opportunity — is not to deny the reality of talent or the significance of superior advanced education, but to provide funds so that the boy of real talent may get as good an education as he needs. To meet the argument that the job of the colleges and universities is to make anyone who has the "will power" a first-rate lawyer, doctor, engineer, or scientist, one must daily educate the American people about the realities of human nature. In such education the analogy with athletics to which I have already referred is not without its value. But equally important is the emphasis on the social equality of a great variety of occupations.

As matters seem to be moving now, the economic rewards are no longer at all commensurate with the

length of advanced education (if they ever were). I
trust it is not too utopian to hope that we can look forward to the day when in a typical American high school
boys and girls will determine their future educational
plans largely in terms of their ability and their real
interests, not in terms of parental wishes or of monetary
and social ambitions. A dynamic democracy based on
the American idea of a classless society will gain strength
as our educational system lowers economic barriers and
at the same time provides adequate guidance for youths
of a variety of abilities and ambitions. As we democra-
tize our social attitudes, the true significance of advanced
education will become every day more apparent. Out of
the present chaos something approaching a rational
system of post-high-school education is emerging. We
must see to it that public support of education beyond
the high school is consistent with our democratic ideals;
without diminishing our concern for education for *all*
American youth we must seek more effective ways of
finding and educating talent for the service of the nation.
Only thus can our unique system of public education
provide the maximum strength for an industrialized
democracy in a divided world.

11

SOME PROBLEMS OF AN ARMED TRUCE

In the preceding chapters I have considered some of the educational problems of the immediate future, yet the topics treated are but distantly related to the fact that we are living in a divided world. If the armed truce with Soviet Russia and its satellites could be transformed by magic overnight into an entirely peaceful ideological competition, many of my arguments would stand unchanged. Assuming our desire to continue as a free people moving toward our historic goals, we should still want to expand and alter our educational system along the lines suggested even if the challenge of the Russian philosophy disappeared. One may go even further and say that if nowhere on the globe were there any believers in the Marx-Engels-Lenin doctrine, we should still want to improve our schools and make them a better vehicle for our democracy.

The one assumption is as unlikely as the other. For the next few decades the best we can hope for is an accommodation with a powerful nation of devout believers in the philosophy of Marx as interpreted by Lenin and Stalin. Anyone who has doubts on this score is referred to the factual and sober account of *Soviet Education* by Shore and the very readable book by Crankshaw on *Russia and the Russians*. In planning for the future of the United States, we must assume at best an armed truce until at least the middle fifties and a divided world for a long time to come. For those who recoil from the word "planning," let it be recalled that all education has to make assumptions about the future; they may be in terms of *status quo*, or of a planned change directed toward a goal, or on the assumption of an unknown cataclysm. If the Soviet philosophy (as I shall continue to call the 1948 Russian version of the Marx-Engels-Lenin doctrine) were purely for Russian consumption that would be one thing. But even a superficial examination of the writings of the proponents shows that its inherent nature is far otherwise. This has been brought home rather suddenly to some people in this country by the events in Czechoslovakia of early 1948.

We are living in a world divided by the impact of a social philosophy the equivalent of a powerful new religion; this doctrine motivates the action of many courageous, ruthless, and quick-witted fanatics. The essence of the belief of the Soviet group is that they are at war with all peoples who do not accept their gospel and that they are bound to win. Unlike the Mohammedan-Christian conflict of earlier times, force of arms is not the primary instrument on which they must rely. Their prophets have said otherwise. Military force is only one aspect of their policy. The totalitarian socialistic regime (the dictatorship of the proletariat) when once established by revolution, will be subject to counterattacks by the armies of the bourgeois democracies according to the orthodox prediction of the prophets; therefore, there must be military power for "defense." At what point this type of defensive thinking when coupled with offensive political action becomes true aggression is one of the metaphysical riddles troubling liberals in the democracies today.

The riddle is troublesome because it reflects the paradoxical nature of the clash between the Soviet philosophy and the progressive democratic doctrines of this country. Both use the same words so often and mean such different things! For the class-conscious Tory of the old school (if there be any left), the ideological conflict presents few difficulties; he never believed in democracy or the people or liberty anyway, so there can be no mistake about *his* opposition to the Soviet views. On the other hand, the average American who has his own very definite ideas about democracy, equality, and freedom, finds the words and attitudes of the leaders of Russia and the satellite nations confusing. The rulers do not pretend that they are in control of a communistic state and yet they preach communism; they talk sincerely about freedom, and yet run a ruthless police state; they endeavor to obtain control of a country by using the machinery of "bourgeois democracy," and then once in control throw it overboard and still talk about democracy with a straight face!

In reports to the *New Statesman and Nation* from

Prague in March 1948, R. H. Crossman (by no means a reactionary observer) has written as follows:

> But the fact remains that three weeks ago Czechoslovakia was a country with civil rights and Parliamentary institutions. Today that is no longer true. When I said this to a young Communist he replied, "But it's such a small price to pay for a great leap forward to socialism!" . . . An hour and a half with Mr. Slausky, the Secretary of the party, showed me clearly enough that he felt for Parliament what Cromwell felt when he said: "Remove this bauble." "How can you call this democratic?" I asked him. "Of course it's democratic. We have succeeded in purging *all* the parties of *all* their reactionaries." "And the newspapers?" "But there, too, we were constitutional. The Cabinet had unanimously passed a law that only recognized political parties should publish newspapers. We are keeping strictly to that rule. But now all the parties are reliable."

This sounds not only like nonsense but the worst kind of hypocrisy. Perhaps it is both, but the evidence points strongly in the other direction. I am convinced that when we are dealing with the followers of the Marx-Engels-Lenin-Stalin line we are dealing with dangerously sincere people. Not that lying to the enemy is a forbidden weapon among them — quite the contrary; but when they speak publicly they are speaking for home consumption. Furthermore, the justification for their actions in terms of democracy is entirely consistent. Turn to Lenin's *State and Revolution* written in 1917 and see how accurately it forecasts the events of March 1948, in Czechoslovakia. A century ago in 1848 in the *Communist Manifesto*, Marx and Engels wrote,

"We have seen above that the first step in the revolution by the working class is to raise the proletariat to the position of ruling class to establish democracy." This is quoted by Lenin, and from this and similar texts the use of the word "democracy" in the modern Russian sense is made absolutely clear. The Communist party in Europe promises not communism tomorrow but a totalitarian socialism — the dictatorship of the proletariat (the first phase of the communist society according to Marx as interpreted by Lenin); in this period the rule is "from each according to his ability, to each according to his *work*." Only at a later day when there are no longer enemies of the proletariat (that is, enemies of those who rule in the name of the proletariat) can force be dispensed with, only then does an unbending dictatorship gradually disappear and "the state wither away." When that utopian day arrives, the "higher phases of the communist society" will be achieved and society will automatically receive "from each according to his ability" and give "to each according to his *needs*"; or so at least runs the party dogma. When the battle is won, so the story goes, not only will milk and honey flow, but the rule of force will disappear; there will be paradise on earth for all.

To deal with a person or group of persons intelligently one must have some idea of their presuppositions. Whether you take an optimistic or a pessimistic view of the chances of turning an armed truce into a peaceful competition of ideologies, the fact remains that we must deal in one way or another with the fanatic yet capable followers of Lenin. Therefore, it behooves us to understand them. I repeat what was said in the concluding section of the chapter on the university — we must study the Soviet philosophy, we must examine and debate the creed of the Communist party as it has been formulated and defended both here and in foreign lands. Indeed, I would go so far as to say that this is the number one educational need of the present moment. This must clearly involve adult education even more than school and college if an effect is to be produced within the next few years. If I were dealing with adult education (as one should in a book on education), I would place as the twin objectives of discussion groups, radio programs, and evening classes an understanding of the American democratic society and its historic goals, and a dissection of the Soviet philosophy and an exposure of its methods. One of the chief problems of the armed truce is to achieve the second of these objectives in the face of the tendency of certain leaders to confuse a tightening of military security with a witch hunt.

One special set of problems in education which arises from the armed truce, then, concerns the study of Soviet philosophy. Both the urgency and the difficulties arise from the nature of the international situation. A second set of educational problems can be defined as the study of other countries and world problems. Old-fashioned isolationism is dead. The children now being educated, as citizens of the United States, will be involved in one

way or another with what is going on in distant countries in a way our grandfathers could never have imag-
ined. A knowledge of world geography, of European
history, and of the culture of the Far East must be provided to some degree at every level of the educational
process. One of the very difficult problems is how some
knowledge of these complicated matters, involving a
mass of detailed facts, can be supplied as part of a general education.

Those educators who since 1941 have been urging a
greater emphasis on the study of foreign nations because
of a belief in the possibility of world government in
the near future have been wrong, according to my
view, in their premise but right in their pedagogic conclusions. Even in a peacefully divided world, the next
generation of Americans must be more intelligent about
other nations and far less parochial in their outlook
than their predecessors. If one hopes, as I do, that
within fifty years the deep cleavage now dividing the
world will become only a relatively shallow ditch, the
children now in school may live to see the day when the
present arguments for world government may not be
entirely fantastic. Therefore, as so often happens in
educational controversies, all hands may agree on what
should be done in practice. The debate which in this
instance boils down to a sharp disagreement about the
time involved may well be suspended.

Finally, we come to the impact of the military situation in an armed truce on our educational system. In-

deed, I might say on our whole life. Those who criticize the present foreign policy of the United States most severely do so in connection with plans for building up the military potential. Before discussing the relation of these plans to education one may be permitted perhaps to give his own appraisal of the necessity for rearmament of this country in terms of an armed truce which may be very long.

As I have already indicated more than once, I am convinced that there is little or no analogy between the Nazi menace and the Soviet challenge. The former, to my view, had to be met by force of arms because it was an immediate military threat. The latter is an ideological and political thrust supported by military means; the Russian armies hidden behind the Iron Curtain are defensive troops to support political gains by the advanced fifth column within another nation; they are not to be used as the spearhead of the forward movement. I recognize I am being very dogmatic about a highly debatable subject. Not only will many experts on foreign affairs disagree with this diagnosis, but history may prove me wrong within the next few months. However, I am bold enough to predict that, unlike Hitler, Russia will not take aggressive military action by invading a nation without an invitation from a *de facto* government. I make this prediction in July 1948, in spite of the gravity of the situation in Berlin. Recurring periods of extreme tension would seem inevitable consequences of an armed truce. If Great Britain, France, and the United States are firm in their determination to hold hazard inherent in our system has been passed, one may hope for an open discussion of the military answer to Russia's hidden military strength based on her vast man power and her ready access by land to many of the sixteen nations in whose future we have so deep an interest. I do not propose to state here what the balance should be except in very general terms. Since Russia might on short notice overrun Europe with her armies (which as far as we know may be mobilized to spring forward at any moment), our balanced strength should be equally ready to strike. How? With what? From where? These are some of the questions to which we need frank answers. And I cannot believe that this talk would in the least disquiet the dwellers in the Kremlin since they assume (according to Marx) that we will strike them in due course. When these questions have been answered in terms of a total diplomatic-military plan for action to offset the Russian challenge, then debate on preparedness will take a more realistic turn. Until that time comes, as the debates in Congress have made clear, we shall be lucky if we can keep our Army up to the strength required to carry out our acknowledged commitments.

Many educators have opposed the program of Universal Military Training as outlined in the Compton report. I have not been among this group. On the contrary, I have supported the report because it represents a most careful investigation of an extremely difficult subject by a group of distinguished laymen. The Compton report, furthermore, gives none of the misleading

positions recognized as just by world opinion, I dou
if the Soviets will force the issue. The proper patte
for preventing the outbreak of another global war wou
seem to involve readiness to answer coercion by the u
of force coupled with willingness to negotiate at a
time on matters of broad policy.

In an armed truce when there is an atmosphere
deep suspicion and each side imagines that the other
about to break the truce, the chances of hostilities a
great. The less the commanders in the two camps kno
of the disposition of the other's troops — their numbe
and their equipment — the more the suspicion multipli
the greater becomes the alarm that the truce will
broken without notice by a perfidious attack. If th
simplified analogy of two armies face to face in form
days of war be applicable to the present divided worl
one basic fact stands out. As long as we in the Unit
States are in complete ignorance of what is going on
Russia and its satellite nations, there can be no hope
relaxing the tensions of an armed truce. Security beir
what it is in a free country, the Russians must have a
extremely poor intelligence service if they are not qui
well informed as to our military capacity. We might a
well be frank about it to ourselves and to them. W
must assume the worst from the military point of vie
about their readiness and their war plans, and we mus
balance them quite openly with a counterplan.

Of course, frank talk about such delicate matters wil
not be possible in the United States until after th
Presidential election. Once this four-year oratorica

arguments for military training (its alleged educational value, for example). The question may be raised whether the investigation is not now somewhat out of date. The nature of the armed truce is now more apparent than in 1947. Keeping the Army up to strength seems the first requisite. If and when an over-all strategic plan for the armed truce can be prepared and explained to the American people, another approach to the man-power problem must be attempted. The present draft law is surely only a stop-gap; it merely postpones a real decision.

There are arguments in favor of enrolling every boy (no exemptions except for extreme physical disability) when he reaches eighteen or graduates from high school in a national militia for a period of ten years. The local unit of the National Guard would be the medium for his subsequent training which could be accomplished in three or four summer camps of two or three months each, and evening drill throughout the year. Those who volunteered for immediate duty in the Army, Navy, or Air Force would be exempt from this ten-year service, and, in addition, could be given special educational and vocational privileges and ample separation pay. Some such system of training, often referred to as the Swiss method, has been advocated for years by a few college presidents, but has received no support from the military men.

College people, of course, favor such a proposal as it would not wreck a college educational year as does even six months of training. Another advantage of some such scheme would be that in case of war a national service act for everyone under 28 would be automatically in operation. The disposal of man power under emergency conditions should be, of course, in the hands of a civilian commission with complete authority.

Whatever may be the ultimate long-range decision of Congress about the military training of young men, the schools and colleges can and will adjust to it, without question. That there will be a cost in educational terms must be readily admitted. What adjustments in calendars and schedules will be required no one can now say. If the present draft law remains unmodified after June 1949 and if volunteering is not adequate, the education of a considerable number of young men will be interrupted. Whatever plan is finally adopted for recruiting the Army and training the youth, one may hope provision will be made for a review of the entire situation every four years by a civilian commission. This was recommended in the Compton report and seems essential.

Those who oppose rearmament on general principles will, of course, be as much against a huge Air Force as U.M.T., or as much against a Swiss plan as the Compton report. They will be appalled by the idea that we must balance military might across the chasm that divides the world, and ask, how can this lead to anything but war? This is a fair question and should be answered by those who talk in terms of an armed truce. We who believe that war is far from being the inevitable outcome of a strengthening of our military power would argue somewhat as follows: once the sixteen nations under the E.R.P. have shown that they can prosper, their answer to the ideological and political thrust from across the Iron Curtain will be clear. Once our military answer to a possible military thrust from the same direction is definite and convincing, a real stalemate will be evident to all clear-minded men even in Soviet Russia. In January 1948, we must remember, it may well have looked in the Kremlin that history was not only on their side for the long pull but also for the immediate future.

Even a fanatic believer in the Marx-Engels-Lenin doctrine may be able to see a road block when he meets it. If the sixteen nations prosper, the ideological thrust will be neutralized; if our balancing the Russian armies is evident, the stage is set for a frank talk with the Soviet rulers. And what should be the terms? A gradual demobilization on both sides; and the first step in this program must be a raising of the Iron Curtain. I recognize this is a great price for the Soviet rulers to pay, but we must play for the chance that they will eventually be willing to accede. From gradual and open demobilization one may hope in time to come to a gradual disarmament beginning, I hope, with the atomic bomb. But, as things now stand, that is a prospect at least five years away.

In any hopeful prognostication of the future we must remember that an ideological thrust can be answered only in ideological terms which include economic, political, and social as well as ideological components. This is what those who talk in terms of armaments and money often fail to see. But this is where education plays its vital part. This is the point where the dynamic nature of this democracy must be demonstrated beyond doubt or question. Otherwise no degree of armament will suffice. If this be granted, improvement of our schools and colleges must be high on the agenda of the American people.

But before proceeding to summarize the changes needed, I should like to enter a plea of *nolo contendere* to the charge of having omitted many highly important aspects of education. The reader may be reminded that what has been attempted is a study of tax-supported schools. Only in connection with universities have I considered the privately endowed and independent educational institutions. My aim has been to stimulate the voter and the taxpayer to take a greater interest in our public schools. For a hostile attitude based on a blanket condemnation I hope there may be substituted a sympathetic yet critical appraisal of their accomplishments as well as their objectives.

Only by means of the greatest self-restraint have I avoided introducing into this discussion of education a strong plea for the support of our privately endowed colleges and universities. One who has had to deal with the effect of the recent change in price levels on the budget of an institution supported by income from endowment, student fees, and current gifts is under strong temptation to turn any document into an appeal for funds. Like the Red Queen in *Through the Looking-glass*, we have had to run very hard in the last twenty years to stand still. An endowment of ten million dollars in 1928 yielded some $550,000 of income; with a price level of at least some 60 per cent higher, it would require $900,000 to go as far; and with the current return of not better than 4 per cent, this would mean the ten million dollars endowment of 1928 should be twenty-five million in 1948. There are few if any institutions which can show a growth of capital of two and a half fold in the last twenty years. The idea that there are colleges and universities today that are so well endowed as to have no financial needs is either pure myth or wishful thinking. The significance of the independent institution is readily granted by even the most ardent advocates of tax-supported schools and colleges. No one would more regret their decline than those who themselves are laboring for the state-supported universities. The diversity of our educational pattern is as essential as diversity of opinion in this democracy of many creeds and conflicting political traditions.

The above digression on the status of privately endowed colleges may serve to emphasize the obvious dangers to all education of a rapid and continuous rise in prices. Businessmen and economists can discuss the dangers of inflation in terms of the prosperity of the nation. But anyone who directs his attention to educational institutions sees the damage which increased prices cause throughout our schools and colleges. The effect on endowment income in terms of what it can buy is only one aspect of the matter. The havoc comes from the inability of any non-profit institution, whether financed by taxes, gifts, or endowment, to adjust rapidly its sources of income to a fast-changing level of prices. The inadequacy of the pay of teachers in our elementary and secondary schools was turned from a serious problem into a national calamity by the inflation of 1945 to 1948. The remedial measures taken in some states as the result of an aroused public opinion have hardly compensated for increased cost of living. A relatively stable price situation seems a requisite for wise planning of our education, however it may be financed. Quite apart from the effects of inflation on the total economy of the nation, one of the major problems of an armed truce which directly affects education is the cost of living. We must contrive to keep our armament program from starting another inflationary spiral.

Let us assume that prices can be stabilized approximately at the 1948 figure; if rises there must be, they will represent not more than a few per cent per annum. Then we can talk in terms of the amount of public moneys which should be spent for education and consider the tax basis for raising this amount. Assuming further that the social and educational philosophy presented in the previous chapters is acceptable, the relative priorities for educational reforms *which cost the taxpayers money* would be somewhat as follows: (1) bring all elementary and secondary schools up to a minimum standard in terms of adequacy of plant, teachers, salaries, and ratio of teachers to students; (2) improve the guidance program in almost every school and support the research on which these programs should be based; (3) increase the number of two-year local colleges in almost every state; (4) institute a scholarship program for talented youth destined for a few professions; (5) improve still further the elementary and secondary schools and bring them all far above the minimum.

To accomplish the first objective requires increased taxation: either a rise of the local rate or, in many states, the reallocation of state funds. Again I venture to point out that there are states where, since the state aid is small and the supervision slight, very poor schools exist locally, though the average may be high. In some states Federal aid is the only answer, for the reasons set forth in the preceding chapter. Of course, the order of priorities I have given has relevance only in so far as the needs are competing for the same source of funds, as is the case with money voted by the Congress. Those concerned with colleges and universities may well question my assignment of so high a place to the high school and the pre-high-school needs. They might be inclined to put first an expanded scholarship program. The reasons for my preference should be evident from the discussions in the earlier chapters. College teachers are keenly aware of the talent lost because of economic barriers to college, but they are apt to overlook the loss in earlier years. They fail to realize how much good material never comes within sight of a university because of the inadequacies of many of the high schools throughout the United States.

The improvement of the guidance system may or may not require increased funds. Certainly a better integration of guidance with the teaching should be possible in many schools without much increase in cost. I repeat once more, at the risk of being wearisome, that this question of guidance is central to the whole philosophy of a democratic school system which endeavors to make society more fluid. I likewise venture to state again that in many high schools the potential professional talent suffers the most from the inadequacies. I wish some organization identified in the public mind with concern for *all* American youth would take some dramatic action to demonstrate a vigorous interest in the gifted boy or girl. This would serve as an encouragement to all teachers. The schools would be stimulated in a direction which in some quarters has been rather spurned as being undemocratic and old-fashioned. A National Commission for the Identification of Talented Youth has been suggested by one group of educators; the sponsoring of this by public school administrators and teachers would be the sort of thing I have in mind.

Of improvements in the training of teachers and school administrators I have written relatively little — not because I feel the subject of no importance. On the contrary, this is one of the directions in which we must hope for rapid progress. The subject, however, is for the most part too technical to lend itself to exposition in a book designed for the general reader. Public funds and private philanthropy may well be used in conjunction in this area. The sociological study of schools and the communities they serve as well as experimental tests of educational innovations, carefully supervised and controlled, are worthy of support. A national organization operating with private resources might provide funds for research in the whole educational field, and at the same time serve as an informed source of public opinion to assist Federal and state officials in the expenditure of public moneys for the same purpose. In the field of medical research we are now seeing the effectiveness of such a partnership between government and private organizations interested in research.

This concludes the summary of the changes which seem to me imperative if our system of tax-supported schools is to be adequate to the task at hand. Once again I offer my apologies for the important topics which have been omitted. This book is in no sense a comprehensive treatment of the problems of education. My objective has been twofold: first, to show how we may examine public education in the light of our knowledge of the present structure of American society; and second, to set goals toward which we must move continually if we are to achieve unity in this industrial democracy of free men.

Some of my readers may feel that I have been inconsistent in my presentation of the subject. I have argued for minimizing social and economic differentiation; yet, I have repeatedly emphasized the importance of considering a specific school in terms of an analysis of the community of which it is a part. This requires speaking frankly of the stratified nature of our society. To my mind, there is no inconsistency in combining a dissection of the social order with an advocacy of policies which are aimed at making the stratification less visible and the entire situation far more fluid. Indeed, one may question whether one can be an effective advocate of change without being at the same time an unshrinking analyst of the present. If this be true as a general rule, education is hardly the field for the exception. To be well founded an educational philosophy must be part and parcel of a comprehensive social philosophy. This is particularly true in the United States at the present moment. Our free schools both reflect the ideals of the nation and insure the perpetuation of our special forms of democratic living. In short, this is why I have related public education and its future to our survival in this grim world.

*　*　*　*　*　*　*　*

Following each war there is a period of reaction, of doubt, of questioning, of murky hindsight as to how the catastrophe might have been avoided. Individually and collectively man is unable to sustain himself for long on a high plane of moral exaltation. Today far too little is said as to the mistakes of United States foreign policy after World War I and in the twenties; far too much is whispered which implies that it was mad folly to have challenged the Axis powers by "actions short of war." As an antidote to this type of reasoning, we would do well to place before our eyes a picture of the twentieth century which might have been. Every morning when we awake we might envisage the kind of United States in which we would be living if Hitler and the Japanese now held the predominance of power.

As the various accounts of campaigns and battles are now unfolding in the hands of historians, it becomes increasingly plain how close was the margin of our victory. Without any reflection on the heroism of our fighting men or the brilliance of their leaders, we can still feel that we have much to be grateful for in the errors of our foes — military errors, strategic errors, technical errors now revealed as we study the documents of Germany and Japan. The months after the fall of France were in the nature of a nightmare even for those who followed the news from the safe distance of three thousand miles. In retrospect we still wonder how it happened that the Nazi tide failed to submerge the British Isles. Why was the invasion postponed? Did the postponement spell the ultimate failure of the German armies? We can clearly recognize now that the Battle of Britain was the turning point of the war. We marveled then at the British victory; it seems no less miraculous now when we know of the desperate odds against the Royal Air Force and the slight reserves of material resources. After Pearl Harbor, in spite of grievous loss, the success of American forces was almost continuous even in the face of unfavorable conditions. Time and again the calculated risk was taken; time and again almost without exception a victory was won.

"How shall we behave ourselves after such mercies?" wrote Oliver Cromwell describing his military triumphs in Scotland. In attempting to work out with factious politicians and embittered fanatics the basis for a republic, the Puritan general repeatedly raised the query: Will our actions prove that we are worthy of the victories God has given us?

Without subscribing to Cromwell's theology, or debating his role in English history, we must feel the force of his question even if we recast it in modern terms. Have we the patience and the courage, the ability to see beyond our own selfish noses, the requisite traits of character to make the United States the living and vital leader among other nations of free men?

In some quarters, nothing but pessimism is in fashion. Atomic bombs and other new methods of warfare, we are told, will soon be upon us in another global war. No one can say this is impossible. Perhaps the fated task of those of us now alive in this country is to develop still further our civilization for the benefit of the survivors of World War III in other lands. It would not be an inglorious mission. But I for one refuse to assume any such outcome of our present labors. To do so would be to renounce already the victories granted to the Allied arms. A behavior commensurate with our mercies (to hark back to the seventeenth-century phrase) would seem to require all of us to be prepared cheerfully for the worst, but determined to do our utmost to make the opposite come true.

A long protracted struggle between two cultural patterns seems to be ahead. But democracy as we understand the word in the United States will, I believe, win almost every round — provided, of course, that we have sufficient intelligence and foresight to recognize the true nature of the struggle. If we are willing to continue to strengthen the sixteen nations whose needs the Congress has recognized under E.C.A. and fortify the democratic forces within those nations, the omens will be favorable for peace in the coming years. Provided further that we neither talk nor act as though we were merely seeking allies for an inevitable war. This nation, having arrived at a stage in history where the words "foreign policy" take on new meaning, must traverse that narrow knife-edge which divides supineness from belligerency. Patience and yet more patience, strength and wisdom to handle strength, a belief in the importance of the historic goals of our unique society, intelligence and courage to cope with problems of terrifying complexity — all these we shall need in abundant measure.

Nothing is static in a period like the present. The United States fifty years from now will be unlike the

present or the past. Our aim is surely to preserve the
maximum degree of individual freedom and at the same
time widen the opportunities for a rich and fruitful life.
The influence of our example, if we succeed, will be felt
throughout the world for centuries to come. Nothing
short of the complete destruction of Western civilization
can obliterate the effects of a demonstration by the
United States in the next ten years that a "government
by the people and for the people" is possible even in a
distraught era following two global wars. Nothing short
of the worst of the fears of the alarmists can vitiate the
endeavors of the citizens of this country to bring our
society nearer to our historic goals.

No one can deny that the people of the United States
in the last century and a half have made a lasting and
highly significant contribution to the development of
civilization. But the task is nowhere near completion.
We have been the medium for carrying forward certain
ideals and aspirations. To a considerable degree it is in
our hands today to decide how much greater shall be our
contribution. Who could ask for more than to be given
an opportunity to live in a time when such possibilities
lie ahead? This is the answer to the current philosophies
of defeatism and despair.

The stream of history is fed by many rivulets and
springs; until the river disappears, each source can claim
its share of credit for the mounting power. But it has
been given to some people at certain times, as it were, to
open a mighty sluiceway. The waters they have liber-

ated soon lose their identity, but the sudden swirl of the new currents has become legendary with the course of time. So it was with the Greeks more than twenty centuries ago; so it is with the democratic nations of the world today, and above all with this republic of free men. Our unique contribution is not in abstract thought nor in art nor poetry. It is rather in a demonstration that a certain type of society long dreamed of by idealists can be closely approached in reality — a free society in which the hopes and aspirations of a large fraction of the members find enduring satisfaction through outlets once reserved for only a small minority of mankind. To bring us still closer to this reality should be the aim of educators in the United States. To assist them in this undertaking, all thoughtful citizens might well rally to the support of public education. For only by their labors can this vast instrument of democracy be made responsive to the needs of a free nation in a divided world.

INDEX

INDEX

A. F. of L. Convention Committee on Education, 37
Accumulated knowledge, relation to human satisfactions, 53
Adult education, 82, 200, 216
Advancement of knowledge, 171–172
Aesthetic judgment, snobbery in, 80
Agents of foreign powers, 174
Agincourt, Battle of, 40
Agnosticism, 96
Agricultural colleges, 161, 163
Agriculture, 123
Air Force, 222
American creed, inherent factors in, 34
Americanization, of foreign-born, 12–14
Analysis of educational problems in sociological terms, 71–73
Anthropologists, analytic approach of, 51; social, 147; standards of, 177
Anthropology, 93, 98, 121; as aid to national leaders, 36
Anti-Semitism, 66, 67
Archaeology, 123, 126
Archimedes, 123
Aristocracy, 11
Armament program. *See* Rearmament
Armed truce, 17, 172, 174, 211; as basis of enduring peace, 2; inherent nature of Soviet philosophy, 212–215; educational problems of, 216; impact of military situation, 217–224

Army, American (1945) and Prussian (1914), 56–58
Art, study of, 77, 83, 86, 108, 135; as forms of personal experience, 84
Artists, creative, encouragement and support of, 78
Arts and letters, leisure class and, 80
Arts and sciences, graduate schools of, 164
Astronomy, 116, 126, 131; Copernican, 130
Athletics, intercollegiate, 166
Atomic bomb, 25, 223, 232
Atomic energy, 50
Atoms, reality of, 129
Authority, hierarchy of, 54
Axis powers, defeat of, 18

Bachelor of general studies, 201
Bacon, Francis, 123, 125
Bar, responsibility of, for future, 34
Basic skills, teaching of, 132
Battle of ideas, 179
Behavior, adult, as test of general education, 98–100, 110–111; of man as social animal, *see* Man, study of
Behaviorists, 101
Beliefs, diversity and tolerance of, 96–97
Benelux proletariat, 24
Biases, in social science, 177–178
Bill of Rights, 3
Biological sciences, 115, 116, 123, 149, 150, 171

Representative government, American adherence to, 3
Research, in physical and biological sciences, 171
Rewards and incentives, in free society, 60
Royal Air Force, 231
Ruling class, 26
Rural areas, educational disadvantage of, 45–46
Russia. *See* Soviet Union
Russia and the Russians (Crankshaw), 211–212

Sabotage, 174
Sacrosanct nature of the individual, 106
Santayana, George, 120
Satellite states, of Soviet Russia, 24
Scholarships, 169, 170, 171, 182, 206, 227; Federal program, 194–199
Schools, free tax-supported, in American society, 1; elementary, 38, 70–71, 182, 183–193, 227–228; private, 46, 47, 136–137; high, 46, 136–137; public, 62, 64–66; secondary, 65, 70–71, 183–193, 227–228; denominational, 97–98; of education, 147; improvement of elementary and secondary, 182, 227–228; relation of, to governmental structure, 183–193; local control of, 183–184; expenditure per child and percentage of state income spent for, 188–189
Science, social, 35–36, 52, 97, 107, 121–123, 177–178; physical, 115, 149, 171; natural, 115–117,

120–121, 127–131, 149; study of, 116–120, 135, 138; definition of, 124–125; advance in, and progress in practical arts, 125; general, in public education, 127–131; history of, 130; medical, 176–177. *See also individual fields*
Scientific materialism, 95
Scientific method, 117–120, 121–122, 142
Scientific problems, philosophic background of, 130
Secondary schools, criticisms of, from professional men, 65; general and specialized education in, 70–71; relation of, to governmental structure, 183–193; improvement of, 227–228
Secular education, 94–98
Self-made man, 39
Semi-profession, 162
Shore, Maurice Joseph, 211
Slavery, 11, 15
Small Town (Hicks), 50
Snobbery, avoidance of, 110; academic, 127
Social anthropologists, 147
Social democracy, an American goal, 4, 6; importance of, in general education, 110–113
Social mobility, in Western democracy, 16
Social philosophers, 126
Social process, education as, 38–40, 48–49, 50–53, 70, 113
Social sciences, 121–123; as aid to national leaders, 35–36; in public education, 52; teaching of, 97, 107; biases in, 177–178
Social structure, characteristics of, 54–55; complexity, 55–56, 59;